# SPEAK FREELY

**New Forum Books**

Robert P. George, Series Editor

# Speak Freely

## Why Universities Must Defend Free Speech

Keith E. Whittington

PRINCETON UNIVERSITY PRESS

PRINCETON AND OXFORD

Published by Princeton University Press,
41 William Street, Princeton, New Jersey 08540

In the United Kingdom: Princeton University Press,
6 Oxford Street, Woodstock, Oxfordshire OX20 1TR

press.princeton.edu

Jacket image: TaniaLuz / iStock Photo

ISBN 978-0-691-18160-8

Library of Congress Control Number: 2017958751

British Library Cataloging-in-Publication Data is available

This book has been composed in Adobe Text Pro and Gotham

Printed on acid-free paper. ∞

Printed in the United States of America

10  9  8  7  6  5  4  3  2  1

*For my teachers, colleagues, and students*

# CONTENTS

Preface    ix

Introduction    1

1  The Mission of a University    9

2  The Tradition of Free Speech    28

3  Free Speech on Campus    51

   *Trigger Warnings and Safe Spaces*    57

   *Hate Speech*    77

   *Forms of Protest*    94

   *Student Groups and Outside Speakers*    116

   *Faculty and Academic Freedom*    141

4  Ideological Ostracism and Viewpoint
   Diversity on Campus    161

Notes    181

For Further Reading    199

Index    205

I have made my professional home within academia, and I am immensely grateful for the opportunities that universities have provided me. I am unabashedly an advocate for universities and their place in American life. I am hardly oblivious to the many flaws that can be found in academia, but it saddens me to see them vilified by outsiders who often do not understand (or at least act as if they do not understand) what universities do and how they operate, and subverted by insiders who sometimes do not appreciate the value and fragility of these institutions.

My fit within academia has not always been a natural one. My entry into the great universities on the East Coast put me in touch with my inner Texas populist. My political inclinations might be charitably called outside the mainstream of university faculty. My orientation toward the discipline of political science is from the margins. But I have been fortunate in finding welcoming colleagues, teachers, and friends who exemplify scholarly ideals and who have repeatedly renewed my faith in and passion for the academic life, and I have been lucky to work with students who are thoughtful, interesting, and engaged. I hope that others find universities as welcoming and as stimulating for generations to come, and I hope this book can make a modest contribution toward preserving these great American institutions for future generations of students and faculty.

As I write this, students mix with "outside agitators" in violent protests to silence and threaten conservative speakers at Berkeley, New York University, and Middlebury College. Universities that should stand as bastions of open dialogue and free speech have too often become sites of intolerance and intimidation. Recent years have brought a steady drumbeat of news reports of speakers disinvited or shouted down, of faculty harassed or investigated, of students disciplined or shunned, of signs and displays removed or destroyed. Rather than serving as exemplars of civil engagement among those holding different views and of rational examination of competing ideas, American college campuses have too often become sad displays of excessive ideological polarization and repressive thought control. These are not just problems on one side of the political spectrum. They have become endemic to university life, and the tools of censorship are routinely taken up by all sides in campus debates. The strident insistence that disfavored views be squelched can and has come from any constituency. Unfortunately, these troubles are not confined to just a few campuses. Institutions across the United States have faced their own controversies, and universities in countries spread around the globe are confronting their own challenges in carving out or preserving a protected space for free inquiry into socially and politically controversial subjects. Indeed, American universities remain far better situated in this regard than universities in many other nations around the world.

The debates over the scope and limits of free speech on campus are not matters of concern only to the campus community. A generation ago, as the Soviet empire fell, the model of liberal capitalist democracy was ascendant. The United States stood as the oldest and most prominent example of that ideal put into practice and shone like the proverbial city upon a hill, inspiring a wave of democratization that seemed poised to dramatically improve the conditions under which people lived across the globe. America was, and is, of course, only an imperfect realization of that ideal, but the aspiration for a freer society was widely shared. Those values are under greater pressure today. The wave of democratization has receded, leaving many nations still in the grip of authoritarianism. The generation raised in the years since the fall of the Berlin Wall is shockingly indifferent to liberal democratic values. Even in the United States, a remarkably large number of young people express no special commitment to democracy or civil liberties.[1] The current crisis of free speech on college campuses is both symptom and cause of a larger threat to the maintenance of liberal democracy itself.

It would be a mistake to be overly complacent about American public support for civil liberties, including free speech, but we should also be cautious about rushing into excessive pessimism about the current generation of college students. It has been a routine finding in the public opinion literature going back decades that Americans express high levels of support for the freedom of speech in the abstract, but when they are asked about particular forms of controversial speech, that support begins to melt away. In the middle of the twentieth century, for example, one study found that more than three-quarters of a sample of lawyers thought that university students should have the freedom to invite controversial speakers to campus, but less than half of the general public agreed.[2] When asked whether the government should be allowed to suppress speech that might incite an audience to violence, less than a fifth of the leaders of the American Civil Liberties Union said yes, but more than a third of that organization's members thought that government should have that power.[3] In the

1950s, Americans said they supported free speech, but they also said the speech of Communists should be restricted. In the 1970s, Americans said they supported free speech, but they also said the speech of racists should be restricted. In the 2000s, Americans said they supported free speech, but they also said the speech of Muslims and atheists should be restricted.[4] Current American college students say that speakers with whom they strongly disagree should be allowed to speak on campus. But a majority of liberal college students changed their mind when they were told that such a speaker might be racist, and more than a third of conservative college students changed their mind when they were told that such a speaker might be "anti-American." Fortunately, the evidence suggests that only a tiny minority of college students favor activists taking steps to disrupt speaking events on campus.[5] Public support for the freedom of speech has not always stood firm, and campus debates over the scope of free speech are likely to have large consequences for how Americans think about these issues in the future.

In the months after the federal Constitutional Convention of 1787, Thomas Jefferson wrote to James Madison with some criticisms of the convention's work. From his diplomatic perch in Paris, Jefferson urged his friend to support the inclusion of a bill of rights in the new constitutional text. The anti-Federalists were saying the same thing, and using the absence of a declaration of rights as reason enough for refusing to ratify the proposed Constitution. Madison thought such objections were misguided, if not hypocritical, and doubted that such "parchment barriers" would do much good if government officials or the people themselves turned their backs on liberty. Nonetheless, Madison was willing to grudgingly admit that a bill of rights might be useful, even in a republic where the people presumably cared about preserving their own liberties and had the political tools to do so. Notably, he thought that "political truths declared in that solemn manner acquire by degrees the character of fundamental maxims of free Government, and as they become incorporated with the national sentiment, counteract the impulses of interest and passion."[6] Liberal tolerance and civil deliberation are foundational to the campus community as they are to the political community, and ultimately depend on the sentiment of community members. We sometimes need reminders of our fundamental maxims of free society, and I hope to provide such a reminder here.

I am thankful to those who were able to offer helpful responses to this work, and in particular to Donald Downs, Chris Eisgruber, Ben Johnson, Ken Kersch, Susan McWilliams, David Rabban, Jeffrey Rosen, Reed Silverman, Geoffrey Stone, and George Thomas. I am grateful to David Ramsey and the University of West Florida for the invitation to speak that launched this book, and for the welcoming venue they provided for the free exchange of ideas.

# SPEAK FREELY

# Introduction

"Neither the entire police force available in Berkeley nor the presence of watchful professors . . . could keep in check the riotous undergraduates of the University of California" who had gathered in anticipation of the appearance of a controversial social activist. The local press and university officials had called for the lecture to be canceled, in light of disturbances that had occurred on other campuses, and there had been arrests in the past for disturbing the peace. Nonetheless, an "enterprising student" had extended the invitation and made the arrangements. The speaker had tried to circumvent the protesters by arriving on campus an hour before the announced time and sneaking into the auditorium where the scheduled talk was to be delivered. The "immense crowd" of protesters soon figured out that they had been duped, descended on the lecture hall, and "noisily demanded" that the speaker come out and face them. Instead, the speech went forward with the ticketed audience inside, and the "demonstration dangerously approached a riot at several stages in the proceedings." The

1

crowd charged the front door but was repelled by a cordon of police. Some of the students outmaneuvered the police and found an unguarded back door, forcing the speaker to briefly flee the stage before order was restored. After the talk, as the speaker sold merchandise to fans in the auditorium, students threw things at the police outside. The speaker escaped mostly unscathed but did lose a hat to the mob, and had learned from earlier events "to never wear anything that is worth much" since lost and damaged personal possessions had become routine features of these campus visits.[1] The activist was not the alt-right provocateur Milo Yiannopoulos in the spring of 2017, but the prohibitionist provocateur Carrie Nation in the spring of 1903.

Such boisterous events were relatively rare, but nonetheless newsworthy and embarrassing, episodes on American college campuses in the early twentieth century.[2] In the spring of 1933, the readers of the *New York Times* were dismayed by reports of a more disturbing string of events taking place at the University of Breslau in what was then Prussia and what is now western Poland. Breslau was a hotbed of support for the emergent National Socialists, and many of the university students were enthusiastic Nazis. Ernst Cohn was a young academic star, who had just been appointed to a new chair in law by the faculty of the university in the city of his birth. Students immediately began disrupting his lectures, and police were needed to clear protesters from his classrooms. The university rector announced that he could no longer guarantee the professor's safety, and appealed to the students to respect the "freedom of teaching and to fight with spiritual arms only." The protesting right-wing students responded with a manifesto of their own, declaring that "a new type of German university of a political nature must be built up," and demanding

Cohn's removal from the faculty, as a left-wing coalition of students called for respecting "liberty of opinion and confession." The faculty complained that the new generation of students cared more about politics than about their studies, and suggested that life would be easier if the faculty started scrutinizing the political views and personal identity of new professors so as to avoid upsetting student sensibilities. Despite a temporary suspension of Cohn's class and negotiations between university administrators and student protesters, the protesters immediately returned to disrupting his lectures and the local police were overwhelmed. The students demanded that they should "be free to have the teachers they want," and insisted on the exclusion of "un-German" professors and suspected "Marxists." The administrators caved, Cohn's class was permanently suspended, police withdrew from campus, and order was restored. When Adolf Hitler was appointed German chancellor, the education minister sent word that Cohn had been officially dismissed. He soon emigrated to England, where he restarted his academic career and became a naturalized citizen.[3] Universities could be the seat of diversity and learning, but they could also be perverted into the seat of conformity and indoctrination. Forces both inside and outside the academy could collude to prioritize politics over scholarship on the university campus, to the detriment of both the institution and civil society.

My concern here is with a particular problem on college campuses that is not new but is newly relevant. Free speech in universities has periodically been under threat, and American universities have been fortunate in avoiding some of the worst assaults that have ravaged universities elsewhere. In the early twentieth century in the United States, faculty, students, and alumni struggled over how independent the faculty would be and whether they could profess controversial views that discomforted (the usually more conservative) donors. In the early days of the Cold War, state governments tried to squelch radical voices on campuses. During the Vietnam War, sometimes literal battles raged over the scope and limits of student protests. The details change, but free speech has frequently been a subject of controversy on college campuses, with some members of the campus community urging more freedoms and others advocating for more restraints. Outside interests have regularly involved themselves in those controversies, seeing the fate of free speech on campus as having important implications for social and political disputes being fought elsewhere. Sometimes the pressure for restricting campus speech has come from the right and sometimes from the left. Sometimes the cry for restricting speech comes from parents, donors, and administrators, and sometimes it has come from students and faculty.

Free speech on college campuses is perhaps under as great a threat today as it has been in quite some time. We are not, of course, on the verge of returning to the rigid conformity of a century ago, but we are in danger of giving up on the hardwon freedoms of critical inquiry that have been wrested from figures of authority over the course of a century. The reasons for this more censorious environment are myriad. I will not try to detail those threats to free speech here. Although some still deny that there is a significant threat to speech on campuses, that position requires an almost willful blindness to what has been happening on college campuses big and small. I will not try to convince you that free speech on American college campuses faces significant challenges, nor will I try to detail for you the many examples of efforts to restrict campus speech, nor will I try to untangle the various forces that drive these contemporary speech debates. These are all important inquiries, but others have done valuable work investigating them.

I take the existence of a serious debate over the scope of free speech in American colleges as a given, and I hope to provide some reasons for resisting the restriction of speech. There are important disagreements over the proper scope of free speech in American society in general, but the college environment raises these issues in a distinctive way and in a particularly important context. As we think about appropriate limits on free speech, I fear that we have sometimes forgotten the purposes of speech on campus. By recovering the purposes of free speech in the university, I hope that we can better evaluate proposed limitations on speech and consider the potential dangers associated with those limitations.

Although I approach these issues with a background in American constitutional law and history, my concern here is not primarily with developing the legal argument in favor of speech on campus. The First Amendment is designed to restrict the power of government officials, not private actors. It constrains Congress, not Facebook; it ties the hands of administrators at the University of California at Berkeley, but not those at Middlebury College. For public universities, university administrators are government officials and constrained by the same constitutional rules that limit the discretion of other government officials. For private universities, those constitutional rules do not apply so directly, though many campuses have voluntarily embraced very similar understandings of free speech. There is a body of law surrounding the idea of academic freedom, and courts have worked to think through how to apply general constitutional principles to the unique context of institutions of higher education.

Those legal arguments can be informative, but my interest here is more fundamental. Laying aside the question of whether courts might enforce some outside body of constitutional rules to limit the discretion of university administrators, how should members of the academic community itself understand their own interests in the free speech debate? What principles should the members of a university community— administrators, faculty, and students—strive to realize on campus? Universities have been called "First Amendment institutions" precisely because of their important place within civil society, a place "where ideas begin."[4] If we hope to sustain institutions that can play that role within American society, we need to act to preserve them as bastions of free thought and critical dialogue.

The argument I want to develop here is that we should understand free speech as central to the mission of a modern university. The editors of a college paper recently emphasized that "the founding fathers put free speech in the Constitution as a way . . . to protect individual citizens from the power of the government."[5] That is certainly true, but the implication that we need not concern ourselves with principles of free speech outside the context of government power does not follow. The right to free speech is not an extrinsic value to a university that has to be imposed by outside forces to serve ends that have no immediate connection to the goals of higher education itself. Rather, the value of free speech is closely associated with the core commitments of the university itself. The failure to adequately foster an environment of free speech on campus represents a failure of the university to fully realize its own ideals and aspirations. Sacrificing speech subverts the very rationale for having a university and hampers the ability of universities to achieve their most basic goals. If we value what universities do and the role they play within American society, then we must likewise value free speech in universities.

In these pages, I hope to provide some reasons for valuing robust protections for free speech on campus and for distrusting proposals to empower campus administrators to police speech on college campuses. As is discussed below, the "speech" on campus takes a wide variety of forms, and they do not all raise the same issues nor should they all be judged by the same standards. Scholarly discourse in the classroom and in academic research should be evaluated by academic standards, and members of the faculty should be held to the expectations of their professions. Scholarly speech is not "free" in the sense of anything goes, but the ideal of academic freedom emphasizes that members of the faculty should have the independence to exercise their professional judgment and not be constrained by social, political, or financial pressures to shade how they teach or what they write. But the campus is home to more than the work of scholars. Universities have long offered an arena in which students and visitors engage with and advocate for ideas. Those debates are often boisterous and freewheeling. They reflect the chaos of American democracy rather than the decorum of the seminar room. What holds those two worlds together is a common commitment to taking ideas seriously, to exploring the unconventional and the unexpected, to examining critically what we might otherwise take for granted, and to holding accepted truths up for challenge and reconsideration. If universities are to be a space where ideas are held up to critical scrutiny and our best understanding of the truth is identified and professed, then dissenting voices must be tolerated rather than silenced, and disagreements must be resolved through the exercise of reason rather than the exercise of force. As it happens, those habits of skepticism, tolerance, and deliberation have value not only for advancing the mission of a university but also for reinforcing the foundations of a liberal democratic society.

I develop this argument for valuing unfettered campus speech across four chapters. First, I need to unpack a bit what I take to be the core mission of a university in order to lay bare the connections between that mission and free speech. Second, I offer some reasons for valuing and protecting speech. The rationale for protecting free speech that I offer here is in many ways conventional, even traditional, but the general reasons for protecting speech can be too easily obscured and forgotten in the midst of particular controversies, and it is important to remind ourselves of why we are better off giving a wide scope to free speech. Third, I apply these considerations to some of the specific contexts that have given rise to controversy of late. In doing so, I hope that a reminder of what we are trying to do on college campuses and the values that free speech serves will allow us to clarify a bit how we should navigate the particular controversies that confront us. Finally, I consider whether university communities should worry about fostering "viewpoint diversity" on campus and just how free-ranging academic inquiry should be.

# 1

# The Mission of a University

Let me begin with a basic but potentially controversial proposition: the modern university is one of the great achievements of American civilization. We do not often, at least anymore, speak of an "American civilization." Perhaps that is appropriate in a commercial republic such as our own. As a nation, we have always celebrated the practical and the popular. We elevate as heroes inventors and businessmen like Thomas Edison and Steve Jobs, social activists like Frederick Douglass and Martin Luther King Jr. and statesmen like George Washington and Abraham Lincoln. The art forms we most celebrate are those produced for a mass audience—television, film, pop music. The "ivory tower" is a pejorative, dismissing those who are not sufficiently rooted in the practical strivings of the day-to-day. The historian Richard Hofstadter once called our attention to the anti-intellectual tradition in American life and the frequency with which public figures have had recourse to the denigration of expertise and specialized knowledge, preferring a more populist "horse sense" to the opinions of elite "eggheads."[1]

But there is an American civilization nonetheless, and universities occupy an important place within it. Commentators have sometimes struggled to capture an "American mind" that is both uniquely American and also elevated. The Victorian English writer Samuel Butler observed that "America will have her geniuses . . . but I do not think America is a good place in which to be a genius," a view that was shared by many of his American contemporaries.[2] Boston's Henry Adams looked across the Mason-Dixon line and concluded that "the Southerner had no mind; he had temperament."[3] The essayist Paul Elmer More returned the favor, dismissing the "half-civilization" that New England had pilfered from old England.[4] The conservative literary scholar Richard Weaver bemoaned returning in the fall of 1939 to the campus of Texas A&M University and its "rampant philistinism, abetted by technology, large-scale organization, and a complacent acceptance of success as the goal of life."[5] Such conservative critics of the American scene as Adams and More could be too pessimistic, even as that scene appeared in the early twentieth century. But over the course of the twentieth century, cultural institutions have flourished in America, creating new homes for the exploration of ideas and values, and universities have been among the most important and successful of those institutions.

This is not to suggest that the modern university does not have problems or confront challenges. Universities are expensive. Although the economic value of a degree remains substantial, the traditional educational model is costly to maintain, and universities have taken on many more expenses in an effort to serve their various constituencies and to entice students to enroll. Those difficulties are exacerbated by public disinvestment from many institutions of higher education.

Both the value and the cost of education give rise to worries about student access. Making the benefits of universities available to an ever-increasing number of students raises not only questions of cost, however, but also difficult issues of adequate student preparation for what universities have to offer. The traditional role of faculty in guiding university decisions has been threatened by the rise of professional administrators and contingent instructional staff, and universities are tempted to sacrifice their core mission by enticing distractions ranging from semiprofessional sports to economic investments. Students, employers, policymakers, and competitors question whether ivy-covered universities remain relevant in the twenty-first century. Perhaps most disturbing is an apparent crisis of confidence among members of the general public in the value of universities in American society. In recent years, Americans who identify with the Republican Party in particular have developed sharply negative views on the contribution of institutions of higher education to the United States.[6]

Despite such causes for doubt, American universities remain the envy of the world. Students from across the globe flock to American universities to pursue educational opportunities unrivaled by anything available in their home countries. The faculties of American universities have dominated the ranks of Nobel Prize winners because they provide a welcoming home to scholars from across the world and the resources and freedom to allow those scholars to push the boundaries of human knowledge. The system of higher education in the United States offers an unmatched diversity of institutions and educational models. A historically high proportion of the population of the United States have earned college degrees, and those numbers continue to grow. The economic value of a college degree continues to rise as well.[7]

These achievements are surprisingly recent, however. It is easy to be lulled into complacency by the long history of many of our most prestigious colleges. Institutions like Harvard, Princeton, and Yale can boast of foundings that predate the formation of the United States itself. But the fact of the matter is that those colleges were for much of their history quite different from what they are today. The colleges of the early republic were more finishing schools than research universities, and they emphasized rote memorization more than critical thinking skills. The modern American university as we know it today was the product of the late nineteenth century. The established institutions of New England that were founded to train ministers were forced to remake themselves into very different institutions, and they were joined by a proliferation of new schools, from the land-grant universities of the Midwest to the new private universities endowed by the Gilded Age elite to the smaller technological, religious, and progressive institutions that carved out unique niches in the collegiate landscape. These modern universities became crucial drivers of economic growth and cultural enrichment over the course of the twentieth century. The modern American university has been with us for only a little over a century. Universities have proven adaptable to social and economic challenges in the past, but there is no guarantee that they will continue to serve the same important functions in American life into the future.

In order to consider how free speech is central to the mission of a university, we must first understand what the mission of a university is. This requires abstracting a bit from the specific situation of any given university. The mission statement of a university tries to identify the core commitments and central goals of that particular institution. Such a statement needs to be abstract enough to encompass the complexity of the institution and allow for changes over time, but it also needs to be specific enough to help an institution set priorities and guide its day-to-day operations. Part of the wonder of higher education in America is its diversity, and there are important differences between Caltech and Sarah Lawrence, between Swarthmore College and Liberty University, between Princeton University and the University of Texas, between Spelman College and the University of West Florida. Such differences will drive individual institutions to make their own peculiar decisions that will shape their community and practices, distinguish them from their peers, and provide a unique experience to their students.

Despite this diversity, modern American universities share some fundamental features in common. From those commonalities, we can see the core mission of the university in general. While identifying a common mission at that level of generality might not help any given institution decide what academic majors to offer, what faculty to hire, or what residence halls to build, it does help identify what an institution must be committed to in order to fit within the framework of a modern university.

At heart, the mission of a university is to produce and disseminate knowledge. Not every university can or should want to do that in the same way. No university seeks to produce knowledge simply, or disseminate it indiscriminately. Choices must be made about how to advance that general mission, but all universities are recognizably engaged in that common enterprise of advancing and disseminating knowledge.

Each part of that formulation is important, and they are inextricably linked in a university environment. The production of knowledge is as integral to the purpose of a university as the dissemination of it. The production of knowledge is, of course, at the heart of the scholarly profession. The scholar embarks on a lifelong journey of learning. That scholarly work might, in the first instance, revolve around the accumulation and synthesis of the existing stock of knowledge. Throughout human history, a critical task has simply been to realize and preserve what is already known. The scholar must pick up the pieces of the scattered bits of knowledge that have been gained in the past, consider the connections between them so that they can be fitted together, and think through their implications for the present age. The first step in the production of knowledge is remembering what has come before.

Learning what there is to be learned can, in the best of cases, generate new insights, new discoveries, and new knowledge. The quest of scholarship, frequently frustrated, is to advance the frontiers of what is known, to learn not only what is already known but also what is not yet known. Pushing the boundaries of what we can know and understand about the natural world, the social world, and the human condition is at the heart of the scholarly enterprise. Universities certainly are not alone in seeking to produce knowledge, but they have been a critically important site for research across a wide range of human endeavors. Moreover, at their best universities are dedicated to the task of gathering, preserving, and advancing human knowledge not for the sake of achieving some other goal, but for its own sake. The struggle to cure a disease, or manufacture a product, or turn a profit can and does lead individuals and organizations to advance the frontiers of knowledge, but such research is ultimately a secondary by-product of those activities and only an instrumental good. Universities are committed to the advancement of human understanding for its own sake. They rest on the proposition that rewards will come from that work, but they encourage the exploration of the unknown without any prior expectation of what those rewards might be. No doubt, there are many intellectual dead ends along this path of progress, but there are also many unexpected gateways to new frontiers. The academic community is dedicated to unbounded exploration, recognizing that there will be many failures, but hoping that there will also be many breakthroughs that could not have been anticipated when the journey began.

Universities are equally committed to the dissemination of knowledge. The scholarly work of producing knowledge is inescapably bound up with the effort to communicate what has been learned. The goal of research is not to hide the light under a bushel, but rather to let it shine forth. The fruits of research are to be shared, with other scholars, with students, and with the general public. Although the scholarly life is often imagined to be isolated, even hermetic, the scholarly enterprise is fundamentally communal. It is a community of scholars that preserves the inherited store of knowledge, and a community that seeks to add to that store. New puzzles and their solutions are advanced, assessed, and recognized by individuals working in a constant dialogue with their peers. Scholarship is a conversation, a conversation that extends across generations and across the globe, and to shut oneself off from that conversation is to shut oneself off from the scholarly enterprise itself.

As a consequence, universities are dedicated to the task of accumulating and sharing our collective knowledge of the world and fostering an environment of constant learning. To do so, universities organize a wide variety of activities to spread the fruits of research. From sponsoring scholarly journals and academic presses to organizing conferences and lectures to maintaining archives and libraries, universities seek to promote the sharing of what has been learned with both a local and a global community of scholars who will in turn make use of and contribute to the common store of knowledge. It is a community that grows rich through the free exchange of ideas.

This community of learning is not limited to those who have dedicated their lives to scholarship. What is gained through research is to be shared not only with other researchers, but also with students and beyond them with the public. Research and teaching are sometimes portrayed as competing goals, but that is true only in a narrow sense. An individual's time is pressured by the competing demands of teaching and scholarship, and undoubtedly some individual scholars have a comparative advantage in one or the other. But most professors know that teaching and research are mutually reinforcing. The best teaching is informed by the latest research, and the challenge of teaching at the college level is determining how to synthesize the mass of research on a given topic and make it accessible for a nonspecialist audience. Academic research should eventually make its way from the pages of a scholarly journal read by relatively few to the classroom where it can be heard by many. Likewise, research is often spurred on by experiences in the classroom. As teacher and student together work through scholarly puzzles and what is known about them, the teacher often leaves those conversations with new insights and a new appreciation of the material, and new thoughts on how those questions might be pressed further. The classroom too is a place of discovery, and not just for the student.

Everything else that universities do flows from this twin mission of generating and disseminating knowledge. Universities are great engines of economic growth. But those benefits are natural products of universities pursuing their core mission of producing and disseminating knowledge. Universities are ill-suited to working as economic agents. Nonetheless, by performing their core function, universities have played an important role in technological innovation and economic growth in the United States and elsewhere over the past century and more. Universities do not and should not focus on maximizing quarterly earnings or bringing new products to market, but they lay the foundations for economic gains. They help build the capital that entrepreneurs leverage to enhance the welfare of society. They perform the basic science that becomes the building blocks of new technologies that reshape the world.

As parents and students are increasingly aware, universities are the training ground for the high-skilled workers needed in the modern knowledge economy. Across their working lives, those who graduate from universities earn a substantial income premium over those who do not, and as a consequence universities have played an important role in lifting generations of Americans out of the economic circumstances in which they were born, and setting them on a new economic path. But much would be lost if universities were reduced to credentialing services for the professional classes. A university degree is worth something because of the intellectual, emotional, and social experiences that universities impart. If those experiences were devalued or debased, then the degree would be worth very little no matter how attractive the campus or elegant the framed diploma.

Universities are incubators of ideas that help shape American society, but their primary purpose is not to mobilize social movements. Universities give free play to new ideas about the wide range of human endeavors, from the sciences to the arts. They shelter dissidents and innovators, idealists and critics. Within universities, scholars question what we think we know about how the world works, about the foundations of society, about the qualities of a well-lived life. Such scholars are not always right, of course. But they expect their ideas to be vigorously debated, to be investigated with both skepticism and care. They push their colleagues and students to reexamine their own assumptions and commitments, and sometimes their unorthodox ideas migrate beyond the ivied walls of the college campus and help remake the daily lives of people far removed from the university.

Universities are critical molders of democratic citizens, but creating better citizens is a by-product of universities performing their primary mission of educating students. Democratic government puts extraordinary demands on the average citizen. Democracies ask individuals not only to earn their living, care for their families, and obey the law, but also to help form public values, set the direction of public policy, and choose the officials who manage public affairs. Universities help produce not only the economic, social, and political leaders who will guide American life, but also the mass of voters who wield decisive power within a republic. Universities help prepare young adults to be thoughtful and responsible contributors to civic life.

Admittedly, our secular research universities might come closest to fitting the model of higher education that I have just described, but I believe the entire array of colleges and universities in the United States and elsewhere can find common ground in the basic commitment to produce and disseminate knowledge. Teaching institutions necessarily prioritize the effort to educate students over the effort to expand the boundaries of human knowledge. The military academies have a foremost responsibility to prepare their students to enter military service rather than civilian life. Religious institutions may well place boundaries on the quest for truth, having a prior commitment to certain revealed truths that are not to be questioned. Perhaps some secular institutions might commit themselves to a similar but political mission, insisting that the members of their communities endorse an implicit statement of faith in order to remain members in good standing. Such qualifications shape particular institutions and give them their distinctive character, but to the extent that they qualify the central mission of a university to engage in skeptical inquiry in pursuit of the truth, there might well be ramifications for the scope of free speech on such campuses.

In order to realize this core mission of the university of producing and disseminating knowledge, and the many subsidiary benefits that come from universities fulfilling that mission, a robust commitment to free speech on campus is essential. Universities seek to constitute communities dedicated to experimentation, discussion, and learning. The university should welcome anyone who is willing to join such a community. The university embraces those who enter its campus, saying, "Come now, let us reason together." It must close its gates only to those who are unwilling to accept that simple invitation. Those who wish to maintain a closed mind and a stubborn orthodoxy will find nothing of interest on the college campus. Those who wish to keep an open mind and have their ideas and commitments tested and strengthened will find joy on the college campus.

This conception of the university is relatively modern. The first universities established on American shores had a rather different mission. Their goal was to inculcate orthodoxy. They were not imbued with a spirit of discovery. Their founders and leaders were convinced that the storehouse of knowledge was already full, the final truth was already known. The mission of the university in such circumstances was to pass on to a new generation the inherited wisdom of past generations. This is still an important mission. Those scholars saw their task as dispelling ignorance by the instillation of the truth, and much could be and was accomplished through the fulfillment of such a task.

A university committed to conveying orthodoxy does not require free speech, and the early decades of American universities did not place much emphasis on free speech. The faculty was expected to adhere to approved doctrine, and the students were expected to imbibe it. These colleges were expected to be producers of doctrinally reliable preachers and finishing schools for the sons of the wealthy (and those who aspired to join their class). At their best, professors in these schools served as stern disciplinarians who put students through the paces of a "system of mental gymnastics" (usually in the form of exercises in Latin and Greek grammar and geometric proofs) that were intended to strengthen the minds of future lawyers and doctors.[8] The classical advocates of colleges in America had no doubt of the value of schooling, but their understanding of education was cramped. They were certain that it was learning that separated the ignorant and dangerous savage from the enlightened and industrious citizen, but they understood the critical feature of higher education to be the stomping out of "wrong ideas and impulses."[9] Strict adherence to orthodoxy was the ideal. Intellectual freedom was achieved through the devoted acceptance of received wisdom.

It is no surprise that the new breed of Gilded Age industrialists like Andrew Carnegie, who was largely self-educated and had spent his teenage years earning a living, had little use for the colleges that dotted postbellum America. From his perspective, college students were wasting their time wrestling with dead languages instead of learning in the "school of experience" as he had done. A college education was "fatal" to those who wanted to be a success in business.[10]

A new generation of education reformers responded by creating the modern American university. Old colleges like Harvard, Yale, and Princeton were radically reformed. New colleges, both private and public, from Carnegie and Cornell in the East to Wisconsin and Stanford in the West, grew up in the new model. Over the course of a few decades around the turn of the twentieth century, such varied figures as Harvard's Charles Eliot, Princeton's Woodrow Wilson, and Johns Hopkins's Daniel Coit Gilman took a lesson from the more academically vigorous German universities to shake up the sleepy American colleges and make them simultaneously hospitable to the life of the mind and relevant to a new age of American enterprise.

The core value of the modern American university would be free inquiry, not indoctrination. It was in this environment that the idea of academic freedom emerged, for it was in this environment that academic freedom would have a purpose. In the reformed university, liberalism, democracy, and meritocracy would ideally go hand in hand. Colleges should fling open their gates and seek to "help all who are worthy to get in," as the president of the University of Illinois declared.[11] The worthy were to be defined not by their wealth, breeding, and willingness to engage in mental gymnastics and adhere to established truths, but by their eagerness and ability to challenge inherited verities, to improve the studies of their fellow scholars, and to place our collective wisdom on firmer foundations. The University of Michigan's long-serving president James B. Angell tentatively reached toward the new ideal when proclaiming that "no man worthy to hold a chair here will work in fetters," and the university should "never insist on their pronouncing the shibboleths of sect or party." The "intellectual freedom of the teachers" was an essential condition for instilling "catholic, candid, truth-loving habits of mind and tempers of heart" in the students.[12] The path to reform was often a rocky one. The First Amendment scholar Alexander Meiklejohn was forced out of the presidency of Amherst College early in the twentieth century because his desire to shake up the "country club college" and instill a sense of American life lived "beautifully, courageously and honestly" did not always sit well with the more conservative alumni and faculty. Meiklejohn favored a new breed of faculty with the "tendency to substitute discussion for pure lecturing, the disposition to lead the students into original inquiry and speculation rather than to preach dogma to them," whose classes could be described as "ordeal by battle."[13] The unsettling educational goals and methods of reformers like Meiklejohn were not always welcome, but in time they made American colleges vital centers of intellectual activity and more relevant to the progress of the nation.

Some would question whether modern universities are truly dedicated to the unbiased pursuit of truth, and as a result they question both the reality and the wisdom of intellectual freedom where indoctrination rather than free inquiry prevails. When Secretary of Education Betsy DeVos complained that university faculty "tell you what to do, what to say, and more ominously, what to think," she expressed long-standing conservative concerns that the modern universities had abandoned their stated mission of rigorously seeking after knowledge.[14] If the faculty were preaching rather than teaching, then it was the intellectual freedom of the students that was being put at risk, and the faculty would have destroyed the necessary preconditions for their own claims to academic freedom. The newly graduated William F. Buckley, the founder of the con-

servative magazine *National Review*, came to national prominence at the opening of the 1950s with his book-length indict-
ment of his alma mater, Yale University, and the "superstitions
of 'academic freedom.'" Buckley thought it evident that the
faculty and administrators of Yale in the early days of the Cold
War did not in fact maintain "an atmosphere of detached impartiality with respect to the great value-alternatives of the
day." The theory of impartiality "has never been practiced" in
the classrooms and corridors of Yale, and consequently cries of
"academic freedom" were just a fig leaf to cover faculty prose-
lytizing of left-wing values.[15] Now, ultimately Buckley doubted
whether an attitude of academic detachment was either possible or desirable when it came to such basic matters as whether
atheism or Christianity, collectivism or individualism, coercion or freedom were correct, and thus he preferred that Yale
shift its "bias" so as to conform with rather than contradict the
commitments and values of its alumni and trustees and of the
citizenry of the United States. But it is notable that the first
step in his argument was to try to show that Yale had failed to
live up to its own core values. If the university were to be an
instrument of propaganda, it could at least have the grace to
pick the right side.

The response of some academics to such charges is to embrace them, and to argue that the universities must act as a
countercultural force of resistance to mainstream political and
cultural values. This idea is not a new one. In the 1960s, Herbert Marcuse, the favored philosopher of the New Left, laid
out the case for rejecting what he called "pure tolerance," or
the tolerance for all sides on contested issues of science, art,
and politics. Such tolerance might be reasonable, he thought,
if the people were capable of rationally evaluating the arguments that they heard. But in the context of a liberal capitalist

society, he thought that was never the case. The people were too "indoctrinated" to recognize the truth when they heard it; they could not be expected to tell the difference between "sense and nonsense."[16] Tolerance is valuable only to the extent that it leads to "liberation," which means that true tolerance "must always be partisan—intolerant toward the protagonists of the repressive status quo."[17] Establishing a real "freedom of thought" necessitated "new and rigid restrictions on teaching and practices in the educational institutions which, by their very methods and concepts, serve to enclose the mind within the established universe of discourse and behavior."[18] In short, progressives should practice intolerance "toward the self-styled conservatives, to the political Right," and recognize that "the majority is no longer justified in claiming the democratic title of the best guardian of the common interest."[19] Since this philosophy of liberation "presupposes the radical goal which it seeks to achieve," there was no reason to hear from those who would question that goal or the means to achieve it. Freedom would be achieved only by "radical minorities . . . minorities intolerant, militantly intolerant and disobedient to the rules of behavior which tolerate destruction and suppression."[20] As the legal philosopher Brian Leiter recently pointed out, however, even Marcuse thought universities were an appropriate arena for tolerating diverse perspectives, and there are good reasons for thinking that Marcuse did not appreciate the depths of the reasons why that should be the case.[21]

There is room in the world for institutions that explicitly embrace intolerance. Let a thousand flowers bloom. Such advocates of intolerance might struggle to convince legislators or wealthy alumni that they should patronize their mission of radical political indoctrination or persuade parents and students that a limited intellectual horizon was the best preparation for life in the modern world, but there is room for them in the marketplace of ideas. It must be recognized, however, that owning the label of "tenured radical" undercuts not only the justification for free speech on campus but also the very mission of the modern university to produce and disseminate knowledge.[22] It presupposes not only that everything worth knowing is already known, but also that education should be dedicated to the achievement of a preordained political goal. The office of minister of information is useful if truth is expendable when politically inconvenient, but it has no place in an institution dedicated to genuine learning.

Some would argue that the mission of the modern university has simply changed, or at least is not strictly focused on the production and dissemination of knowledge as I have posited. The notion of an "engaged university" sometimes points in that direction. In 1999, a group of university presidents signed on to a "declaration on the civic responsibility of higher education," which called on colleges to "renew our role as agents of our democracy."[23] Such ideas are hardly new. The postwar president of the University of Chicago famously challenged Americans to become better educated, for "the death of democracy is not likely to be an assassination from ambush. It will be a slow extinction from apathy, indifference and undernourishment."[24] Various individual institutions include in their mission statements a commitment to molding democratic citizens, shaping the character of students, or engaging with their communities. The implications of such commitments can be various, from "service learning" programs to civic education. Often they have been tied to social justice concerns, such as Occidental College's self-described mission of offering a curriculum with a "multicultural focus" and a "deeply rooted commitment to the public good."[25] Such initiatives inspired

Stanley Fish, an outspoken literary scholar and former college dean, to grumble that members of the faculty should "save the world on your own time."[26]

In the abstract, the idea of an engaged university committed to "educating citizens" can draw interest from both the political right and the political left. It would be relatively uncontroversial for universities to try to foster such civic virtues as honesty, integrity, empathy, curiosity, individual responsibility, and critical thinking. Some on the left might be more leery of a university likewise trying to foster the "nationalistic chauvinism" of patriotism, just as some on the right might object to a faculty dedicated to teaching "an emancipatory form of citizenship" aimed at "eliminating oppressive social practices" and "constructing nonalienating social relations."[27] For some, the very purpose of a university is to "change" the world, "to create, maintain, and continually develop the Good Society."[28] Few would object when newsman Walter Cronkite intones in promotional videos for the University of Texas, "We serve a place as big as it is diverse. Maybe that's why we're so single-minded in our purpose: to help transform individuals into the thinkers, dreamers and leaders of tomorrow. What starts here changes the world."[29] Things become more controversial, however, when what some would call the "pedagogy of freedom" or the "pedagogy of solidarity" turns out to be what others would call teaching "students how to organize protests, occupy buildings, and stage demonstrations."[30] There is little doubt that some on American college campuses are, in fact, committed to a view of the university mission and of their own role within it that creeps toward the latter description.

While recognizing that quite genuine point of disagreement, however, we should not lose sight of the inescapability of "ethical advocacy" in at least some parts of the university curriculum. Some worry that this can tip into mere "preaching about values," and argue that faculty should be skeptical of providing students "with *the* truth about the important issues we study." From the perspective of the university as a whole, however, we can recognize that none of us are likely to have a firm grasp of "*the* truth," while expecting faculty to urge students toward what they take to be correct, if contested, answers to some hard questions. Urging students to be "independent thinkers" can be compatible with faculty passionately advancing their own views of the matters at hand.[31] The difficulty comes when faculty or students seek to stamp out critical engagement with those ideas and censor out competing perspectives.

I do not believe most academics embrace the role ascribed to them by DeVos and Buckley, or urged upon them by Marcuse and his heirs. Most understand their work to be guided by the principles laid down by university reformers over a century ago. Within the domain of their particular professional ambit, most faculty seek to pursue the truth as best as they can, in a spirit of open inquiry and disciplinary rigor, and to introduce students to that enterprise of discovery and to the fruits of the labor of the many researchers who have likewise embarked on that journey. It is because they embrace those ideals that free speech is crucial to what they do, and the tradition of free speech on campus is a worthy tradition to preserve. Much would be lost if the minority of faculty, students, and administrators who reject those ideals are allowed to reshape the universities, and if others remain on the sidelines as mere spectators as the prized universities that were built over generations are gradually dismantled.

# 2

# The Tradition of Free Speech

If the production and dissemination of knowledge constitute the central mission of a modern university, then how is free speech related to that mission? Is free speech a pleasant (or unpleasant) add-on that we could easily remove without doing any real damage to the institutional integrity of the university itself? I think not. If we were to sacrifice free speech on college campuses, we would be subverting the core values and very purpose of a modern university. We would be left with an institution that looked something like the modern university, but that was no longer dedicated to the basic task of a university and was no longer concerned with preserving the practices and habits of mind that make universities valuable institutions.

In considering this argument, I will draw on some of the lessons of American constitutional law, but I should be clear that the key question is not what the First Amendment to the US Constitution or other constitutional provisions require. To be sure, as governmental agencies, public universities in the United States are bound by federal and state constitutional requirements, and those constitutional rules limit what policies state universities can adopt. Private universities, however, have more legal flexibility to chart their own course, though most have voluntarily adopted policies and principles that mirror core First Amendment requirements. Of course, universities outside the United States have no concern with the First Amendment at all. But legal requirements are largely beside the point.

Free speech is important to universities because it is constitutive of the institution, not because it is imposed as a legal restraint by an outside force. Small children might play with a chessboard and chess pieces, but if they do not adhere to the rules governing how each particular piece can move across the board, they are not playing chess. The rules of the game are constitutive of the game itself. Likewise, free speech is bred into the bones of a modern university, and any institution that sets those principles aside can no longer be meaningfully regarded as a proper institution of higher education. It would have become something else, and whether that something else is attractive is for others to judge. I have no interest in such a faux university. Unfortunately, there are some colleges in the United States and elsewhere that are in danger of becoming shells of their former selves, mere facades that camouflage a campus culture that has rejected liberal tolerance and free inquiry in favor of dogma and indoctrination.

Free speech is constitutive of a modern university because the principles of free speech are tools critical to sustaining the project of intellectual inquiry that expands our knowledge and conveys that knowledge to others. Universities need to provide a wide scope to free speech not because they need to secure the preconditions of the democratic process and free and fair elections, or to check government power, or to provide opportunities for authentic self-expression.[1] They need to protect free speech because that is how scholars can make progress in refining our understanding of the world and in improving the understanding of others. Constitutional doctrines can be helpful for thinking through those principles, but they are not exhaustive of them. The First Amendment is generally understood to protect freedom of expression for a variety of purposes, and truth seeking is only one of them. For universities, however, free speech is valuable precisely because of its utility in generating, testing, and communicating ideas.

In particular, I want to draw on two strands of thought on why free speech is critical to the scholarly project. The first strand is primarily legal and political and is found in the Jeffersonian advocacy of democratic dissent at the turn of the nineteenth century. As the party of opposition in the new republic, the Jeffersonians found themselves pioneering the argument for a robust conception of free speech, and their legacy has reverberated through American political life and constitutional thought ever since. The critical lesson learned from those early debates in the years after the founding was that even if we were in agreement that there was bad speech, we should be exceedingly cautious about empowering any official to play the role of the censor in order to identify and suppress that bad speech. In practice, the decisions of how to apply the power to silence speech would be made by fallible individuals, and we could not safely rely on the enlightened officials using the power wisely.

The second strand is primarily philosophical and is found in the liberal tradition that developed a powerful defense of liberty of thought and liberty of conscience. This is not the liberalism that defines one side of contemporary political debates. This is the liberal tradition that drove back feudalism in

Europe and elevated the values of individualism, liberty, the rule of law, and democracy. The development of those arguments directly paved the way for the founding of the American republic in the late eighteenth century, the reformation of American universities at the end of the nineteenth century, and the explosion of constitutional jurisprudence protecting speech in the twentieth century. Reacting against the system in which political and religious authorities routinely suppressed dissent and enforced orthodoxy, liberal thinkers argued that humanity would be better off if individuals were freed to hear competing ideas and to make up their own minds. A society that was intellectually free would be generally more free and more just than one that was intellectually fettered.

To elaborate on the first, Jeffersonian, strand of thought: The nation's founders were convinced that free speech was essential to republican government, but they did not have well-worked-out ideas about what the principles of free speech might require. Their experience with republican government was too limited. They knew that the kind of governmental licensing of authors and printers that English poet John Milton had railed against more than a hundred years before the American Revolution was incompatible with liberty, but they had not yet had occasion to think much beyond that. As a practical matter, the press had been relatively unrestricted in the American colonies, and the founding generation took the freedom to engage in raucous debates over matters of public concern more or less for granted.

The first serious controversy over the meaning of free speech in America did not come until a decade after the adoption of the US Constitution, but that controversy wound up having dramatic consequences for how the freedom of the press was understood. The founders had hoped that political parties would not develop in the United States. They thought parties disturbed the public peace and elevated partisan interests over the public interest. By the end of George Washington's presidency, their dreams of a republic without parties had already been shattered. In the 1790s, a Republican opposition led by Thomas Jefferson and James Madison organized against the policies favored by the Federalists who held the White House first under Washington and then under John Adams. Their disagreements were aggravated not only by their general fear of partisan factions and division over domestic policy, but also by the events in Europe. The terrors of the French Revolution raised new fears about the excesses of democracy, and the United States struggled to remain neutral in the war between France and England. The two nascent parties found themselves as divided over foreign policy as they were over domestic policy, with the Jeffersonians favoring the French and the Federalists favoring the English. The Jeffersonians soon began to fear that the Federalists were soft on American independence and sympathetic to monarchical government. The Federalists in turn feared that the Jeffersonians were eager to join the Jacobins and throw the country into social revolution and mob rule.

In this highly combustible environment, the Federalist majority in Congress passed the Alien and Sedition Acts of 1798. The Alien Acts gave the president sweeping powers to expel noncitizens living in the United States, and the Sedition Act made it a federal criminal offense to publish or say anything "false, scandalous and malicious" that might bring the federal government or federal government officials into "contempt or disrepute" or excite against them "the hatred of the good people of the United States." Notably, the vice president of the United States, who happened to be Thomas Jefferson, was not protected by the terms of the statute. The act was set to expire just after the elections of 1800.

The Sedition Act was, in many ways, consistent with inherited understandings of the requirements of a free press. The act did not establish a board of censors or require authors to receive a license before publishing their work. Publishers were free to print whatever they wanted and speakers were free to say what they liked, but they were liable to criminal punishment if they misused that freedom and wrote or said things that the government found objectionable and dangerous. The crime of sedition laid out in the 1798 congressional statute had long been recognized in English and American law, though it had not been previously codified in federal legislation. The Federalists had even liberalized the English law by making the "truth of the matter" published a valid defense at trial. The traditional English law of seditious libel allowed punishment for any statement that was damaging to public order, regardless of whether it was true. The new American law promised to punish only false statements. Within the English and American legal tradition, individuals were at perfect liberty to speak, publish, or act in ways that did no damage to other individuals or to the general public. But an individual's liberty ran out as soon as that person's actions did harm to someone else, and what could be more harmful than to excite the hatred of the good people of the United States against the president or members of Congress? Hate speech was not "free speech."

The Federalists did not mean for the Sedition Act to be a mere symbolic gesture. Prosecutions were organized out of the office of the US secretary of state. Jeffersonian newspapers were shut down, and their editors were jailed. A particularly cantankerous Republican congressman found himself incarcerated for a fiery speech he had delivered to his constituents.

Federalist judges declared that this was perfectly consistent with the new US Constitution. The Republican-controlled state legislatures in Virginia and Kentucky passed resolutions denouncing the Sedition Act as unconstitutional, and Federalist-controlled state legislatures adopted resolutions of their own praising the law and rebuking the Republican states for daring to suggest that Congress might have violated the Constitution. Freedom of the press became a rallying cry of the Republicans as they prepared for the elections.

As a practical matter, the constitutional validity of the Sedition Act of 1798 was settled by the election of 1800. The Jeffersonians swept the Federalists out of power, capturing both chambers of Congress and the White House and several statehouses as well. For the first time, the country witnessed the peaceful transition of power in the national government between partisan opponents. The Jeffersonian Congress did not renew the Sedition Act, and the president pardoned those who were still incarcerated under the terms of the act. A Federalist Supreme Court justice who was particularly aggressive in enforcing the act was impeached, in part for his conduct in sedition trials. The Federalist Party was never again competitive at the national level. The Sedition Act came to be viewed as a fatal miscalculation by the Federalists, and the practical meaning of the freedom of speech in America was expanded.

For our purposes, I want to call attention to two features of this episode as relevant to thinking about contemporary debates about free speech on campus. First, the Sedition Act debate highlighted that the distinction between true and false or good and bad speech was not adequate to protecting free speech. The Federalists promised that they wanted to punish only purveyors of fake news, but the Jeffersonians thought that would likely be a slippery slope. Truthful statements would be suppressed because no one could be confident that they could "establish the truth to the satisfaction of a court" and thereby be secure from punishment.[2] The fear of prosecution would chill even truthful speech. Moreover, mere opinion would be branded as false and, "in the present temper of parties," the accused would be unable to convince a court that what they had said might be true.[3] Empowering some to judge for everyone else what speech was worthy of a hearing risked significantly shrinking the public sphere. Those currently in control of government might benefit from exercising such a power, but everyone else would be made worse off by the incumbents' ability to filter out speech that they found disagreeable or dangerous. No matter how well intentioned or well drafted the policy, once the power to suppress speech was granted, it tended to expand in ways that aided those who held power and hurt those who were powerless. The only safe way to protect the powerless was to bar anyone from punishing speech.

Second, the Sedition Act experience raised doubts about whether there are ever likely to be neutral arbiters to evaluate highly contested speech. "Real liberty," one Federalist congressman insisted, did not include "a license to injure others."[4] Few disagreed with that point in the abstract, but the difficulty was determining what counted as injury to others. Lawyers in the early republic were generally comfortable with that legal standard, which was applied in lots of contexts, but in the politically controversial context of sedition prosecutions any sense of general agreement about how to apply it broke down. While the Federalists might insist that an "honest jury" or judge could distinguish between protected speech and speech that caused harm, the Jeffersonians doubted that any such honest jury could be found. It was unavoidable, they thought, that those who were asked to preside over sedition trials would be partisans and "interested in the issue."[5] When Federalist news-papers could declare, "It is *Patriotism* to write in favour of our government—it is Sedition to write against it," there could be no fair trials under the Sedition Act.[6] The Jeffersonians actual experience under the law seemed only to confirm those doubts. The lesson that Americans learned at the end of the eighteenth century was that no one could be trusted with the power to suppress or punish controversial speech. Good intentions to suppress only bad speech counted for little when there was significant disagreement over which particular speech was good or bad. The power to limit speech would inevitably be abused. The only safety was to err on the side of liberty and let the people themselves hear all sides and weigh the value of the speech.

The second notable strand of thought comes from the liberal tradition. The liberal tradition of free speech actually begins with a related claim that not coincidentally also found its way into the First Amendment, the liberty of religious conscience. There is a basic structural similarity to many arguments for the liberty of conscience and for free speech because both are concerned with a similar goal. As the Protestant Reformation roiled Europe, many struggled with the putative authority of the church to establish Christian dogma. There was often a close relationship between church authorities and legal authorities, but the defense of liberty of conscience was fundamentally aimed at carving out a zone of privacy within which individuals and voluntary groups of individuals could develop their own ideas about the requirements of their religion and dissent from orthodoxy.

The liberty of conscience was first and foremost a liberty to seek the truth. For writers like the English poet John Milton, the English philosopher John Locke, and the American preacher Roger Williams, the stakes could not be higher. At the end of the day, discovering the truth about religious obligations was a matter of individual salvation. Those who failed to do their absolute best to seek the truth risked eternal damnation. In the face of that danger, a liberal tradition was born arguing that freedom of thought was an essential condition for making progress toward reaching the truth. The arguments for enforcing conformity and stifling dissent were rehearsed by religious and legal authorities, but the advocates for freedom eventually won the day. The advocates of order, like the Puritan minister John Cotton, insisted that "to allow any man uncontrollableness of speech" would necessarily result in some speaking "great blasphemies," leading the weak-minded astray and destroying the civil peace.[7] Without question, those dangers were real. The advocates of liberty insisted that the risks were worth taking. John Locke argued that it was not blasphemy but intolerance that made it difficult for diverse individuals to live together peacefully. He noted that it was less the "diversity of Opinions" that upset the civil peace than "the refusal of Toleration to those that are of different Opinions." In any case the fact that people will disagree, that there would always be a diversity of opinions, was impossible to avoid.[8] The only real question was whether some opinions would be suppressed, and quite possibly whether the truth would be suppressed along with them.

The liberal tradition in time turned its attention to speech generally, and was soon arguing that religious conscience was not a special case. Dissenters of all types should be tolerated. Perhaps the greatest single monument in this tradition was the publication of John Stuart Mill's little book *On Liberty* on the eve of the American Civil War. Mill was born in London, early in the nineteenth century, and subjected to a demanding course of study by his father, himself a well-known philosopher. Mill soon became one of the most notable liberal reformers in England and one of the most important thinkers of the nineteenth century, with celebrated works on logic, philosophy, political theory, economics, and women's rights. His book on liberty has perhaps had the greatest long-term influence and offered a landmark defense of limited government and an expansive realm of individual freedom. It begins with an essay on the "liberty of thought and discussion," which is itself a foundational text on freedom of speech.

It is significant that Mill was not primarily interested in the details of a constitutional text or even legal interference with free speech. England was itself a democratizing country, and Mill admitted that its government in the mid-nineteenth century was less censorious than it once had been, or than the other European states continued to be. Like his contemporary, the French visitor to America Alexis de Tocqueville, Mill was beginning to worry about the oppressive effects of public opinion in an egalitarian society. For both Mill and Tocqueville the "tyranny of the majority" was the emerging danger in democratic societies, but they worried that the majority would make itself felt not only through elections and the use of government power but also through the more subtle tools of social pressure and private institutions. Mill pointed out that the philosophy of self-government did not solve all social and political problems. "The 'self-government' spoken of is not the government of each by himself, but of each by all the rest."[9] What would be needed going forward was not only protection "against the tyranny of the magistrate," but also protection against "the tyranny of prevailing opinion and feeling." He hoped to identify principles that would establish not only the proper limits of governmental power but also the "limit to the legitimate interference of collective opinion with individual independence."[10] If we were to appreciate why liberty, and particularly liberty of thought and speech, was good for us and good for society, then the human race would ultimately be happier and better off. If we were to practice greater legal and social tolerance for dissenters, the nation would flourish.

Mill's argument is particularly instructive to us in thinking about the university setting because of the reason why he thought we should value free speech and give it ample room in our political, social, and cultural institutions. Free speech is essential to the advancement of knowledge. Mill most certainly would not have limited free speech to the college campus. He hoped to see a greater appreciation of dissent and free inquiry everywhere, from the halls of Parliament to the pages of the newspapers, from the pulpits of churches to the parlors of debating societies. In the English intellectual culture of the mid-nineteenth century, it was in those institutions that ideas were seriously discussed. The modern American university strives to take ideas as seriously as did the London Debating Society that Mill helped found.

Mill made several interrelated arguments in favor of society recognizing an expansive principle of free speech. Let me divide them into three here. We might call them an argument from humility, an argument from arrogance, and an argument from conviction.

The argument from humility begins with the assumption that we are all fallible. Those who seek to suppress speech with which they disagree or that they find offensive do so on the assumption that such speech is false and thus not worth hearing. But, as Mill reminds us, "to refuse a hearing to an opinion, because they are sure that it is false, is to assume that *their* certainty is the same thing as *absolute* certainty."[11] We must be humble enough to admit that we might be wrong and those with whom we disagree might be right. Our own ability to realize the truth requires that we keep an open mind and be willing to listen to others who might turn out, against all expectations, to have some useful points to make.

Mill knew that maintaining this attitude of humility would be difficult. Long before we began to talk about information bubbles and media echo chambers, Mill pointed out that we all live within social contexts that deeply shape our preconceptions about the world. From inside the bubble, the views we hold never seem particularly contingent. They seem obvious, commonsensical, and true. It requires some imagination, and even some intellectual bravery, to admit to ourselves that we cannot be certain of what we know, and that it might be useful to really listen to others and not just shout them down. Absolute princes, he noted, "or others who are accustomed to unlimited deference," will rarely hear dissenting voices and as a consequence will all too easily assume that there is no rational basis for dissent. But the tendency to live inside our own intellectual bubble is not limited to princes and others who might surround themselves with obsequious yes-men. It is the common situation of humankind. Even those who are "more happily situated" so as to "sometimes hear their opinions disputed" are not immune from the tendency to simply accept as true the opinions that happen to be "shared by all those who surround them." But the simple fact is that every sect, every nation, every generation is convinced of its own shared opinions, even as those outside the boundaries of those communities think that those ideas are "not only false but absurd."[12] It is easy for the Christian in a Christian nation, the democrat in a democratic society, the liberal in a liberal polity to imagine that their most cherished commitments are obviously true, but those living across the globe or in a different time might well think the opposite and be just as certain in their own beliefs. If we are committed to the pursuit of truth, we must keep an open mind and be willing to question everything that we believe.

Closely related to the argument from humility is the argument from arrogance. Mill's plea in the argument from humility is that we keep an open mind and be willing to listen to those with whom we disagree. His challenge in the argument from arrogance is that we be willing to allow others to hear those disagreements as well. We are not only tempted to close our own minds to disagreeable opinions, but we are also tempted to suppress those opinions so that no one else will encounter them either. In the arrogance of our certainty that we already know the final truth, we gain confidence to silence those who would question us.

Mill's argument from humility, like the early arguments for liberty of conscience, is an appeal to our self-interest. We would be better off if we were to keep an open mind and prepare ourselves for the possibility that we might be wrong. His argument from arrogance is more difficult because the appeal is not to our own self-interest but to the interest of humanity at large. By closing down debate, we deny others the opportunity to make up their own minds about where the truth might lie. If we happen to be correct about the truth of our own opinions, then perhaps the suppression of debate is of little cost. But if we happen to be mistaken, and Mill reminds us that we might easily be mistaken and moreover that we are often blind to our own mistakes, then we have arrogantly damaged others by forcing them to accept our mistaken beliefs as gospel. At the end of the day, we must accept the fact that there is no "infallible judge of opinions to decide an opinion to be noxious [or] decide it to be false."[13] Although we might wish the best for others and for society at large, it is intellectual arrogance to assume that others will benefit only from hearing our thoughts, and not from hearing the thoughts of our opponents. It is oppression to deny them the opportunity to think for themselves.

> However positive any one's persuasion may be, not only of the falsity but of the pernicious consequences—not only of the pernicious consequences, but (to adopt expressions which I altogether condemn) the immorality and impiety of an opinion; yet if, in pursuance of that private judgment, though backed by the public judgment of his country or his contemporaries, he prevents the opinion from being heard in its defense, he assumes infallibility. And so far from the assumption being less objectionable or less dangerous because the opinion is called immoral or impious, this is the case of all others in which it is most fatal. These are exactly the occasions on which the men of one generation commit those dreadful mistakes, which excite the astonishment and horror of posterity.[14]

The more certain we are that we already know the truth, the more abusive we are likely to be to those who have the temerity to question it. In doing so, not only do we block ourselves from following the path of wisdom, but we block others from that path as well.

Finally, Mill offers us an argument from conviction. Here he again appeals to our self-interest but does not even require us to embrace the virtue of humility. How would we even know whether the opinions that we hold dear are true? Mill suggests that the only way we could be confident in our own opinions is if we have seen them weather serious challenge. One way of characterizing the difference between American universities as they existed in Mill's day and modern research universities is that the former relied on rote memorization of orthodoxy and the latter embrace freewheeling debate. Mill had no time for the "mere conformers to commonplace, or time-servers for truth" who were content to repeat the conventional wisdom but unwilling to examine it too closely.[15] Those who wished to be convinced that what they know is true should be willing to engage in vigorous debate with those who had their doubts. Only those who did not really care whether their beliefs were true could afford to shut themselves off from the criticism of skeptics. Some might be content that "if once they get their creed taught from authority," no one be allowed to question it, but Mill pointed out that "this is not knowing the truth. Truth, thus held, is but one superstition the more, accidently clinging to the words which enunciate a truth."[16] Universities should do better than seek to promote superstition, no matter how comforting it might be.

We can advance knowledge only by subjecting our most treasured beliefs to careful scrutiny. While "great individual thinkers" might be able to survive "in a general atmosphere of mental slavery," most of us would suffer in such stultifying conditions.[17] At best, we would find ourselves clinging to ideas "as a dead dogma, not a living truth."[18] For ideas to really take root and become firm, and justifiable, convictions, they must be tested in intellectual battle. All honest scholars should be keenly aware of the weaknesses in their own argument. The most persuasive advocates know their opponent's case at least as well as their own.

> He who knows only his own side of the case, knows little of that. His reasons may be good, and no one may be able to refute them. But if he is equally unable to refute the reasons on the opposite side; if he does not so much as know what

they are, he has no ground for preferring either position. . . .
He must be able to hear [the arguments of adversaries]
from persons who actually believe them; who defend them
in earnest, and do their very utmost for them. He must
know them in their most plausible and persuasive form; he
must feel the whole force of the difficulty which the true
view of the subject has to encounter and dispose of; else he
will never really possess himself of the portion of truth
which meets and removes that difficulty.[19]

Those who seek the truth must be fearless in exposing their
ideas to examination, and perhaps dissection.

If we wish to advance knowledge, we need to seek out diversity of thought and be willing to engage in an honest assessment of the merits of our antagonists' arguments and the de-
merits of our own. "Both teachers and learners go to sleep at
their posts, as soon as there is no enemy in the field."[20] Mill
urges us to wake up from our slumbers. If we wish to learn, we
must venture beyond our own comfortable environs and get
out into the wider, and wilder, intellectual world. "Only
through diversity of opinion is there, in the existing state of
human intellect, a chance of fair play to all sides of the truth."[21]
We should cherish those opportunities to hear from and argue
with those who dissent from our orthodoxy. If they are wrong,
we should be eager to show them to be wrong. If they are right,
we should be eager to learn from them.

Mill was keenly aware not only that we are fallible and
might not have a firm grasp of the truth, but also that even
those who are largely mistaken might nonetheless have some
insights to offer. If we refuse to engage with those who we
think are obviously mistaken, we may fail to see the ways in
which they are not mistaken, and as a consequence we may fail

to improve our own ideas. Our critics do us the favor of taking our ideas seriously and of helping us identify our errors and, we may hope, correct them. As any author knows, such criticism can often be painful to hear, and the more closely held our beliefs are, the more emotionally discomforting it is to have them scrutinized and picked apart. But it is only through that process of honest review that we can have confidence in what we think we know.

Mill did not himself use the metaphor of the "marketplace of ideas," but his arguments link up naturally with that image. Although Justice Oliver Wendell Holmes did not use that specific phrase, he is generally credited with introducing the concept into American constitutional jurisprudence; the context was his famous dissenting opinion in a case involving the sedition prosecution of a group of Russian immigrants who had encouraged workers in a New York munitions plant to stop producing weapons during the First World War. Holmes admitted that it was natural for those who had the power to do so to try to persecute the expression of opinions that they think are wrong, especially when you "care wholeheartedly for the result," but he argued that dissenting opinions had to be tolerated. Like Mill, he counseled humility, for "time has upset many fighting faiths." Rather than putting unquestioned faith in our own ideas, we should recognize that the "ultimate good desired is better reached by free trade in ideas—that the best test of truth is the power of the thought to get itself accepted in the competition of the market."[22] In his confidence that truth would prevail in the free competition of ideas, Holmes echoed John Milton's defense of religious toleration. We should not underestimate the power of truth to triumph, he advised, for "let her and Falsehood grapple; whoever knew Truth put to the worse in a free and open encounter?"[23] The truth did not need censors to fight her battles for her; only falsehood needed the suppression of the opposition to bolster its position.

Not everyone is as optimistic about the power of truth to prevail in the marketplace of ideas. We have all seen examples of individuals and groups embracing bad, and even demonstrably false, ideas. Perhaps truth needs a bit of help in the struggle to win hearts and minds. Certainly the marketplace of ideas does not always operate perfectly or smoothly. Nonetheless, the university is precisely the type of environment where a "free trade in ideas" is encouraged and ideas are placed in "open and free competition." Regardless of how well the marketplace of ideas works in the wilds of the Internet or the streets of New York City, there is good reason to think that universities are closer to living up to the ideal that Holmes had in mind.

Importantly, it is not at all clear that there is much of an alternative to Holmes's "best test of truth" in a fair competition of ideas.[24] Universities are committed to the belief that the best means for advancing knowledge is through the critical scrutiny of ideas, and that the proper goal of a community of scholars is to refine that process for scrutinizing ideas so that it is as effective and as efficient as possible. Rather than sheltering ideas from criticism, scholars seek to face those criticisms squarely and do their best to evaluate their merits. We advance knowledge by putting ideas to the test of arguments and evidence, and by developing habits of critical analysis. While the advance of knowledge is often imperfect, it does not advance at all if criticisms are suppressed rather than investigated.

If universities seek to produce and disseminate knowledge, rather than dogma, then they must foster an environment in which no beliefs are sacred, no ideas are safe from scrutiny, no opinions are immune from criticism. A primary commitment to the pursuit of truth requires that all other commitments always be subject to question. We must be willing to defend our ideas and give a fair hearing to our critics, not for the sake of our critics but for our own sake. The Socratic dictate that the unexamined life is not worth living is the implicit motto of any institution of higher education. The university welcomes all those who wish to honestly examine their lives, their beliefs, their ideals, but it has no place for those who prefer to be sheltered from such searching interrogations.

What Mill sketches out is an extraordinarily inclusive community. It is a community composed of all those willing and able to learn. It excludes no one because of who they are or what they believe. Indeed, it is a community that should strive to draw into itself the diverse world of divergent opinions and perspectives. But it is also a community that puts a high demand on its members. It asks them to shake off their prejudices and preconceptions and be willing to see things afresh and investigate things anew. It asks them to be civil and tolerant, even of those whom they regard as vile and offensive. It asks them to admit that they are fallible and prone to error, and to recognize that they have much to learn from those who are very different from them, and even from those who are very much mistaken. At their best, universities strive to assemble such a community.

At this point, we might introduce a qualification to Mill's argument. Mill himself was concerned with society as a whole, rather than with the particulars of a university setting. Moreover, he was writing near the end of the heyday of the amateur scholar, or perhaps of the gentleman scholar. He was largely educated by his father; he earned his living as a clerk, editor, and journalist, and briefly as a member of Parliament. He was, in modern parlance, a public intellectual, not a denizen of a university community. Although Mill did not try his hand at the natural sciences, like many of his contemporaries he followed his interests wherever they might go. After producing a major treatise on logic, he turned his attention to producing a major work on political economy, and from there turned to political philosophy. When encouraging us to seek out and learn from the unorthodox and the dissenters, he excepted only mathematics, for he thought that in that realm alone is "all the argument . . . on one side" and "nothing at all to be said on the wrong side of the question."[25]

Not long after Mill's death, the intellectual world went through a revolution. Intellectual life within universities was reorganized into disciplines. This was not simply a matter of rearranging the furniture; it marked a new departure in how the acquisition of knowledge was pursued. With the rise of academic disciplines came new ideas about expertise. Debating in the salons of London, Paris, or Boston was no longer good enough. The amateur scholar could no longer be expected to keep up with the increasing specialization of fields of knowledge and the rapid pace of intellectual progress. Scholars and scholarship began to be evaluated not just on their erudition but also on their methodological rigor. Particular fields of study began to develop their own disciplinary ways of knowing, or what the Germans called *Wissenschaft*. The American reformers of higher education at the end of the nineteenth century were greatly influenced by what the German universities had been pioneering in the years before. The systematic pursuit of knowledge required specialized training and dedicated study. Disciplinary boundaries divided up the field of knowledge, scholarly associations and journals were formed, PhDs were awarded, and new expectations for research by university faculty were established.

These developments had important consequences for how we should conceptualize free speech on campus. The demands of expertise require that we discipline free speech. There is a tension between the freewheeling spirit of debate that Mill and others advocated and the careful accumulation of knowledge that modern universities try to foster. As Yale law professor Robert Post has observed, this in part is a tension between the value of democratic egalitarianism, in which everyone should get a fair hearing, and the value of meritocratic expertise, in which those who are thought to have something to add to the scholarly conversation should take priority.[26] The US Supreme Court's interpretation of the First Amendment of the US Constitution has been particularly concerned with keeping the pathways of democratic participation open to all citizens and allowing citizens the fullest scope to hear all sides and make up their own minds on questions of public interest. Free speech on campuses, on the other hand, is geared in part toward training future citizens who can actively and critically participate in that public sphere, but it is especially concerned with setting the conditions under which the frontiers of knowledge can be effectively advanced and the bounty of those explorations can be effectively communicated. Scholars have to work as gatekeepers who try to filter out bad information while letting in good information. Even as universities throw open their doors to all those willing to learn, they must insist that the assembled community of scholars conduct itself with appropriate decorum and rigor. Free scholarly inquiry does not mean a free-for-all.

In sum, we have seen that the truth-seeking mission of universities dovetails with the truth-seeking value of free speech. There are other values that free speech can serve, and does serve, in the broader society. The liberty of free speech exercised in many contexts is primarily about the value it has to the speakers themselves, and not necessarily about the value being provided to the audience. In a free society, we should want to give space to that sort of liberty. When teenagers line up along a parade route holding a banner enigmatically enblazoned, "Bong Hits 4 Jesus," the value in the activity was to be found in their ability to let their freak flag fly, not in the possibility of viewers finding enlightenment from reading the banner. When protesters and counterprotesters line up to scream at each other across a police barrier, they do more for themselves than for any possible audience. A free society should make room for our desire to express ourselves, but universities have a different and more limited mission. Free speech is valued at a university not because it allows individuals to express their feelings. It is valued because the members of the campus community need to be able to engage in a reasoned exchange of views in order to improve all of their understanding of the world we live in. It is regulated and channeled as necessary to advance that important purpose.

Notably, the truth-seeking justification for free speech emphasizes the value of open inquiry and debate to the listener, not the speaker. The speaker already knows what he or she thinks, and while speakers might welcome having the strength of their convictions tested through argument and debate, those who stand the most to gain are the listeners who will be exposed to new ideas and have the opportunity to think through their potency. Universities should strive to make speech available for their members to hear. There may well be value in a liberty of self-expression, but that value is not grounded in our desire to advance knowledge and dispel ignorance. When speech is suppressed, it is the community that suffers from having their intellectual world darkened.

# 3

# Free Speech on Campus

There was no golden age. Free speech on American college campuses has always been controversial and contested. The proper boundaries of free speech have never been clear, and the basic commitment to the principle of free speech has rarely been unwavering. This is not a debate that began only recently, and the advocates of free speech have frequently changed sides. For over a hundred years, alumni, donors, and politicians have tried to stifle professors who challenged their economic interests or offended their moral or religious sensibilities. Student publications have always been treated as a thorn in the side of college administrators. In the 1950s, politicians and trustees sought to purge any whiff of "subversives" from campus, and in the 1960s they turned their sights on civil rights activists. In the 1950s, students complained of an overwhelmingly left-wing faculty, and conservative faculty members pointed to examples of foundations and deans trying to shape the composition of the faculty and curriculum to serve liberal causes. Students have periodically disrupted campus and shouted down speakers.

In the midst of all this conflict and divisiveness, the aspiration toward robust free speech on campus has grown. Universities struggled to gain more autonomy from legislatures and trustees, and to a significant degree succeeded. Professors battled to gain more protections for their ability to pursue ideas wherever they led and to teach students as they thought best, and to a significant degree succeeded. Students fought to gain more autonomy and resources for pursuing their own intellectual, political, and social interests, and to a significant degree succeeded. Supporting all these efforts to expand the scope of campus free speech was a maturing appreciation for the intimate connection between the central mission of the university to pursue the truth and free inquiry and debate as the only possible means for advancing that mission. All members of the campus community came to understand that the power to censor was a mighty temptation, but it was a power that could not be safely entrusted into anyone's hands. Unbridled freedom of speech could be discomforting, baffling, and alarming, but the alternative would drain the universities of any real value and put them back onto the path of decline that threatened their very existence in the late nineteenth century.

Along the way, there have been important markers laid down calling on campus communities to identify and live up to these higher ideals. It was in Germany that the modern ideal of free speech on campus was first developed, and in doing so German universities established themselves as some of the finest institutions of higher education in the world at the turn of the twentieth century. The young scholars who returned to the United States after being exposed to those German universities brought with them a vision of a vibrant community of scholars unafraid to ask hard questions and to face up to hard answers. The German philosopher Friedrich Paulsen influentially sounded the call to arms. "For the academic teacher and his hearers there can be no prescribed truth and no proscribed thoughts. There is only one rule for instruction: to justify the truth of one's teaching by reason and the facts." With that freedom would undoubtedly come much that is "untenable, strange, and absurd," and professors will often expound "foolish opinions," but ultimately "the free presentation of individual thoughts . . . has more life in it and awakens more life than the prescribed presentation of transmitted thoughts." Turning his attention to the emerging social sciences, Paulsen admitted that to the political parties who contested for control of the government, "science is but one of the means of keeping themselves in power by influencing public opinion. With the truth as such the parties have nothing whatever to do; if it is for us, very well, if it is against us, away with it!" But the "people cannot as such have an interest in the preservation of false conceptions"; the people need and benefit from "a proper knowledge of the actual conditions," and as a consequence "can have no desire to place obstacles in the way of an honest search for truth."[1] Paulsen's warning is prophetic. Partisans may always be inclined to value propaganda and dogma over inconvenient truths. Society as a whole, however, must be able to face facts, and universities are a crucial institution for revealing the truth. Universities can serve that critical public purpose only if they are not commandeered by partisans. Ideologues on both the left and the right would like to use universities as a mouthpiece, but the people themselves would benefit the most if universities were independent of any faction and were free to engage in critical inquiry.

The American Association of University Professors was founded in the early twentieth century to advance these principles in the United States. In the midst of World War I, the new organization under the leadership of the philosopher John Dewey tried to clarify what the mission of a university is, and what the responsibilities of boards of trustees and college administrators therefore were. While admittedly some "proprietary schools" might be founded for the "propagation of specific doctrines," whether religious, social, political, or economic, most American universities did not fit this mold. They were instead "untrammeled institutions of learning." Those institutions exercised a "public trust," which could be fulfilled only if scholars were free to pursue their work with "disinterestedness and impartiality." Against the "tyranny of public opinion," the university should serve as an "intellectual experiment station, where new ideas may germinate and where their fruit, though still distasteful to the community as a whole, may be allowed to ripen until finally, perchance, it may become part of the accepted intellectual food of the nation or of the world." At their best, universities could "help make public opinion more self-critical and more circumspect" and train democratic citizens to be more curious and more thoughtful.[2]

In the midst of the civil unrest of the 1960s, the commitment of universities to free speech was tested and reasserted. After a decade or more of repeated assaults on the freedom of scholarly inquiry on American campuses, faculty and students alike strove to reinstill the principles of free speech. When the students in the Yale Political Union invited the segregationist Alabama governor George Wallace to campus in 1963, Yale's president, fearing violent protests and overriding faculty objections, convinced the students to withdraw the invitation. A decade later, student protesters shouted down William Shockley, who had been invited by a student group to participate in a debate. A Nobel Prize–winning physicist, Shockley had become a vocal exponent of the genetic inferiority of blacks and frequently participated in campus debates with the psychiatrist Frances Cress Welsing, who argued that white people's racism derived from their own genetic inferiority. In the aftermath of the Shockley incident, a faculty committee led by the historian C. Vann Woodward produced a celebrated defense of "freedom of expression at Yale." The report declared that "the history of intellectual growth and discovery clearly demonstrates the need for unfettered freedom, the right to think the unthinkable, discuss the unmentionable, and challenge the unchallengeable." Universities had a particular responsibility to uphold a commitment to free expression, to provide "a forum for the new, the provocative, the disturbing, and the unorthodox," and to serve as a bulwark against "authoritarianism," including the authoritarianism of prevailing public opinion. Members of the campus community had an overriding duty to preserve and respect an untrammeled freedom of speech and had no right to obstruct others from exercising that freedom or from hearing the views of controversial speakers.[3]

As student protests roiled campuses across the country in 2014, the president of the University of Chicago formed a faculty committee to consider principles of free expression on campus. The committee, led by law professor Geoffrey Stone, issued a report advancing an expansive commitment to free inquiry within universities. "It is not the proper role of the University to attempt to shield individuals from ideas and opinions they find unwelcome, disagreeable, or even deeply offensive." The university's "fundamental commitment is to the principle that debate or deliberation may not be suppressed because the ideas put forth are thought by some or even by most members of the university community to be offensive, unwise, immoral, or wrong-headed." All members of the campus community are entitled to advance their own ideas, to hear the ideas of others, and to reach their own judgment about the validity and utility of those ideas. Likewise, every member of the campus community and the university itself had a "solemn responsibility not only to promote a lively and fearless freedom of debate and deliberation, but also to protect that freedom when others attempt to restrict it."[4] The Chicago statement, like those that came before it, has met with some controversy. Even as faculty at other institutions, such as Princeton, have adopted its statement of principles as their own, some have pushed back. The conservative National Association of Scholars complained that the Chicago statement did not emphasize enough why free speech was valuable on a university campus.[5] Meanwhile, a student editorial at the University of Chicago complained that the faculty report did not exclude "hate speech" from the scope of campus free speech, and argued that the "students' mental well-being or safety" should take priority over free speech.[6]

Each generation must fight its own battles over free speech on campus, and universities must constantly renew their commitment to their central mission of advancing and communicating knowledge through free inquiry and debate. Those principles have not always been well understood or fully realized. Universities have frequently failed to uphold and defend their own ideals. If universities are to remain valuable institutions in the twenty-first century, however, the members of the campus community will need to preserve the college campus as a sanctuary for serious debate of unorthodox ideas and avoid succumbing to the temptation to make them echo chambers of orthodox creeds. Universities must attempt to organize themselves in a way that allows the campus community to advance the central mission of the production and dissemination of knowledge, and those organizational principles must necessarily include a basic commitment to a robust conception of free speech.

## Trigger Warnings and Safe Spaces

The language of trigger warnings and safe spaces has only recently appeared on American college campuses. The concepts are still a somewhat marginal phenomenon, but are rapidly entering the mainstream. Relative to the actual threat they pose to academic freedom, they have probably received outsized attention. They have become something of a flashpoint to debates on free speech in universities, however, in part because they seem to represent a troubling intellectual orientation. It is worth thinking through a bit why these ideas have provoked such a strong reaction. Doing so might provide us with a useful starting point for considering the challenges to free speech on campus today.

I want to begin by suggesting that there is a reasonable core to both concepts, and that both advocates and critics of them would do well to bear that reasonable core in mind. Like many reasonable ideas, however, they can be abused. The difficulty comes from the abuse of the concepts rather than the concepts themselves. It has perhaps been these controversies as much as anything that have led critics to deride the current generation of college students as "snowflakes" who are incapable of handling the smallest adversity. The label obscures more than it reveals, and we should push past it to take seriously the ideas at issue in these debates.

Let us take up trigger warnings first. Trigger warnings are a form of content warning, with a twist. Content warnings are familiar from mass media. For example, television viewers are routinely warned that the material they are about to see might be suitable only for a "mature audience" owing to its explicit content, violent images, strong language, or adult themes. "Viewer discretion is advised," the audience is warned so that those of a sensitive nature can turn away, or children can be shielded from what is about to appear. Content warnings are designed to address the fact that the mass media reaches a diverse audience, and that consumers should be able to choose the materials to which they will be exposed. More controversially, those same content warnings can be used to classify different materials and make some more difficult to access. Having been labeled as suitable only for a mature audience, an item can then be safely tucked away or removed from circulation so that it will not fall into the wrong hands. But in such cases, what should be objectionable is less the desire for the content warning itself than the use of the content warning to impose further forms of censorship such that even willing consumers are unable to readily access the objectionable material. Content warnings emphasized consumer choice and catered to parents who wanted to exercise control over the media diets of their children, but they could also be a tool for suppressing disfavored art.

Content warnings now have a somewhat antiquated feel. They were seriously fought over when potentially objectionable material was mass-produced and yet potentially capable of being confined. The comedian George Carlin's famous routine on the "seven dirty words" that could not be said on television gave rise to government regulations and judicial decisions in the 1970s precisely because broadcast media seemed unusually intrusive and yet controllable. The parent might not know what was about to be said on the radio, and thus it was thought reasonable that some precautions should be put in place to warn listeners to turn the dial or to confine problematic material to times or channels that were understood to not be suitable for all audiences. But now the comedy routine— and its shocking language—is featured on Wikipedia, and Carlin's performance can be readily found on the Internet to be viewed by anyone carrying a smartphone. Unsurprisingly, Carlin's language no longer seems so shocking, as the culture has adjusted to the pervasive exposure to content that once had to be diligently sought out.

Trigger warnings originated on the Internet and served a comparable function to traditional content warnings. They warned web surfers that the material they were about to encounter might be objectionable to some, and thus urged readers to proceed with caution or turn away entirely. The categorization of content and its rationale were different from traditional content disclaimers. Rather than worrying about the effects on the immature or the decorous, trigger warnings appealed to a therapeutic concern for those who had suffered psychological damage. The rise of the diagnosis of posttraumatic stress disorder (PTSD) brought with it the recognition that exposure to "specific trigger stimuli" could exacerbate symptoms of the trauma, just as external stimuli can trigger the symptoms of various physical ailments from allergies to migraines.[7] Those who suffered from the disorder could find that seemingly innocuous events could result in heightened stress, and patients were advised to identify and manage potential triggers accordingly. Indeed the very diagnosis of PTSD often involves an assessment of whether the patient has a tendency "to avoid situations that might trigger recollections of the traumatic experience."[8] From that specific medical context, the language of trigger warnings seeped into Internet communities that frequently included trauma survivors, such as self-help groups for victims of sexual assault. The trigger warning served as a useful precaution to a specific, but also specifically relevant, set of readers who feared that exposure to particular content might cause them psychological harm.

As sometimes happens, the concept and terminology soon migrated into an ever-wider environment and mutated as it did so. The warnings proliferated on the web and social media, and so a generation of students became familiar with them as ubiquitous features of socially conscious content providers. Having been socialized in an information environment in which trigger warnings were routine, many of those students expected the same familiar warnings to adorn the content they encountered as they entered college campuses. Most immediately, faculty were advised to include trigger warnings on classroom materials that might be deemed risky to some.

In its more restricted form, there is some utility to the idea of trigger warnings, and there are possible models for how to introduce them into the university environment. But even in their restricted form, they raise some difficulties. In the more expansive form in which they have mostly been deployed on college campuses, they become quite troubling.

In its most restricted form, the idea of a "trigger" exists within a medical framework. Those who have a severe allergy to peanuts might have their symptoms triggered by the presence of peanut dust. Those who have PTSD might have their symptoms triggered by something that reminds them of the original trauma. For students in either situation, it would be useful and appropriate to identify what might trigger their symptoms, and it would be appropriate to try to find accommodations that will minimize the risk of harm to them. Warnings of the presence of a potential trigger to the symptoms of their illness might reasonably be part of those accommodations. Campus cafeterias routinely identify common allergens that can be found in the food that they serve so that those with allergies can take appropriate precautions, and students suffering from PTSD could certainly be informed of what materials they could expect to encounter were they to enroll in a given class. Indeed, a standard syllabus lists the subject matter and learning materials of a course, and students should expect instructors to accurately describe the contents of a class.

There is an established model of medical accommodations for students in university classrooms that has become familiar on campuses since the passage of the Americans with Disabilities Act. Students with a range of learning disabilities are regularly assessed by specialized administrators and provided with a uniform set of accommodations that the university has determined is consistent with its own mission and adequate for the affected students to be able to do their work. Faculty members are informed of any necessary actions that they might need to take when those individual students register for their class. Those accommodations, from the use of a laptop on which to take notes during lecture to extra time on timed tests, are tailored so as to allow the student to take full advantage of the academic opportunity without damaging the integrity of the academic program designed by the faculty.

One could imagine that model being extended to include those suffering from PTSD. Individual students could be assessed and appropriate individual accommodations could be deployed with an eye toward both facilitating the student's educational progress and preserving academic standards. Moreover, such a regimen of evaluation and accommodation would take seriously the underlying concern of the discourse of trigger warnings, the possibility that some students are living with mental health difficulties that could impact their ability to take full advantage of their educational opportunities. A modern university dedicated to its openness to a wide range of deserving students should be committed to helping those students manage the obstacles that they might face in navigating the demands of higher education. For many years now, universities have been rushing to commit more resources to providing mental health care for students, and the appropriate accommodation of those suffering from PTSD would fit naturally with those priorities.

Unfortunately, trigger warnings have taken on a much more expansive form on college campuses, and in doing so they have created problems of their own. It is not regarded as sufficient to identify the topics and materials to be discussed in a class; they must be labeled as either safe or hazardous. Third parties, notably students, have taken to calling for trigger warnings not on their own behalf but on behalf of unidentified others who might suffer an unspecified harm from encountering targeted course materials. As a free-floating worry about the psyche of fragile students, the advocacy of trigger warnings drives us toward labeling some course materials as dangerous and as a consequence in need of quarantine. Such readings are not deemed merely to be controversial or offensive, but to have the capacity to cause, or trigger, immediate psychological harm. In the absence of any specific PTSD diagnosis, however, there is no possibility of assessing the relative risks or harms that might be associated with any given text. The discussion is immediately biased toward minimizing the risk of harm rather than evaluating that risk and balancing it against other considerations, such as the intellectual or pedagogical value of the texts in question. Nor does the blanket use of trigger statements attempt to calibrate the accommodation that might be necessary to enable an affected student to fully participate in the course while preserving the integrity of the course as a whole and for other students, and respecting the freedom of faculty to design the courses that best serve their educational purpose.

Removed from the context of an actual diagnosed case of PTSD, the idea of a trigger swiftly loses any meaning. Classically, a PTSD trigger might be anything that happens to remind the particular individual of a specific past trauma. A date on the calendar, a smell, or a sound might all stir unpleasant memories. But once disassociated from any particular case of PTSD, the concept of a "trigger" simply becomes a generic reference to emotionally challenging subject matter. The mere reference to sexual assault, violence, harassment, or natural disaster is sufficient to raise the worry that it might be triggering. Ironically, campus trigger warnings lean into, rather than attempt to ameliorate, what might be clinically diagnosed as PTSD. The tendency of a patient to avoid perceived triggers is typically taken to be a symptom of the ailment. The treatment often involves working to overcome that psychological tendency, to engage and confront and ultimately surmount triggering stimuli rather than to avoid them. In keeping with its origins on Internet discussion boards, the insistence on trigger warnings becomes more about the performance of victimhood than a meaningful effort to help actual victims.

Disassociated from the specifics of a clinically diagnosed condition, the claim that something might be "triggering" becomes an all-purpose means for avoiding or silencing disfavored speech in the name of harm prevention. Literary texts from *The Great Gatsby* to *The Adventures of Huckleberry Finn* have been called inappropriate for college-level reading and discussion because they might be traumatic to students who have experienced sexual assault or racism. Court cases and statutes relating to rape have been deemed too potentially disturbing for law students studying the criminal law to read.[9] At Oberlin College, administrators announced a policy, eventually withdrawn in the face of faculty objections, that urged instructors to remove from their syllabi any text "that could be a trigger" for a wide range of "issues of privilege and oppression" unless it was simply "too important to avoid," in which case the text should be made "optional" for those who wished to avoid reading it so that students would not have "to choose between their academic success and their own wellbeing."[10] At Occidental College, students complained that a Republican student group had created a display of American flags to memorialize the victims of the 9/11 terrorist attacks, arguing that "the American flag is particularly triggering."[11] The display was destroyed by unidentified students soon after it was erected. At Wellesley College, students petitioned the art museum to remove a sculpture of a sleepwalking man because it was a "source of apprehension, fear, and triggering thoughts regarding sexual assault."[12] It was eventually moved to a public park in New York City. With some success, a feminist student organization in Australia has lobbied universities to provide trigger warnings for class materials, and for its own activities insists that members provide trigger warnings before introducing discussions or materials mentioning such anodyne topics as food, spiders, pregnancy, sex, and "slimy things," as well as more common topics such as rape and racism.[13]

In response to such campus controversies, the American Association of University Professors has issued a report critical of trigger warnings. The report anticipated that such warnings would be extended to the materials contained in university libraries, and libraries had long rejected placing "prejudicial labels" on materials for fear that such labels would tend to restrict access and discourage use of those materials. Even in the context of voluntary headings in course syllabi, however, the report objected to the tendency to make "comfort a higher priority than intellectual engagement," which would inevitably tend to drive controversial subject matter out of the college classroom. The proliferation of trigger warnings sidelined the genuine problem of getting adequate treatment for those affected by serious psychological ailments while empowering administrators and activist students to overrule faculty members on the appropriate content of a program of study in an academic discipline.[14]

In constructing courses, faculty must routinely consider how best to expose students to difficult material in order to advance their understanding of the subject at hand. Teachers of constitutional law, for example, must reach some determination of how much they need to expose students to the materials that the government has tried to ban and that courts have had to assess under the First Amendment. For some, it is sufficient to discuss those materials at a step removed, to deal with them in the abstract and to focus discussion on the larger principles at stake in such disputes. For others, however, it seems impossible for students to truly appreciate what is at stake in these disputes unless they are forced to grapple with the materials that were deemed so controversial. Experiencing the visceral impact of offensive materials might be essential to understanding the issues at play. When putting together a casebook on American constitutional law, I proposed including a photograph of a sheriff and a stagecoach robber who had been executed by hanging to illustrate a section on the death penalty. My coauthors, perhaps wisely, thought the image was too much, and we left it out.[15] The social theorist Michel Foucault famously begins his book on the history of the penal system with a vivid description of the public execution of an eighteenth-century would-be assassin of the French king.[16] Must one take an unflinching look at the results of state violence in order to fully examine the issues surrounding it? Experts in the field are likely to differ on that question, but trigger warnings would tend to drive such material out of college classrooms and encourage students to avoid difficult classes and topics.

The Africana studies program at Lehigh University recently launched an initiative for foreign study in Ghana, where students could confront remnants of the slave markets through which African slaves passed before being transported to the New World. As one student who participated in the program observed, "there are no trigger warnings that can prepare you for how you're going to feel when you're standing in a slave dungeon." For those who organized the initiative, an invaluable and unique educational experience depended on "having a very emotional experience in that space."[17] Historians might well believe that students will not sufficiently understand the horrors of the slave experience or racial tyranny if they are not exposed to descriptions and images of the brutality faced by the enslaved or the results of lynchings. While it would seem unwise to toss students unprepared into such emotional maelstroms, it is at the heart of academic freedom that faculty be allowed the flexibility to determine whether and how to introduce such materials. Passing such critical decisions about course content to college administrators risks stifling innovation in teaching and restricting the scope of the educational experience.

The idea of safe spaces has a related but somewhat different origin story. In a therapeutic context, a session was framed as a safe space where patients could let down their guard and reveal their emotional turmoil. From that setting, the concept permeated the broader culture, as epitomized in the title of the best-selling self-help book from 1969 *I'm OK, You're OK.*[18] Although that cultural wave eventually crested and receded, it left a lasting imprint. Notably, it was integrated into the educational ethos of primary school teachers. The classroom, like the therapist's office, was characterized as a safe space, placing a priority on affirming the self-esteem of students. The idea soon migrated into higher education, particularly in courses aimed at exposing students to the challenges surrounding diversity. As one early account of the introduction of a required college class on racism and sexism observed,

> In a class such as this which deals with topics that students find difficult if not threatening, creating a safe space is critical. Students must feel secure that their comments will be treated with respect whether or not the faculty member or the class agrees with them. Students must have confidence that faculty members are in control of the discussion and will intervene, if necessary, to prevent personal expressions from provoking personal attacks by some who may find them offensive.[19]

As that author admitted, however, the need for a safe space had to be balanced with an instructor's obligation "to see to it that blatantly false beliefs are subjected to mature and thoughtful criticism. Striking the correct balance is no easy task."[20]

In practice, striking the correct balance has proven exceedingly difficult. It probably did not help that such classes sometimes veered into mere advocacy and blurred the lines between personal identity, feelings, and ideas. As another instructor of such a course advised her colleagues, it was possible to turn "the class into a consciousness-raising session," characterized by "the sharing of personal experience with others in order to understand the larger social context for the experience and to transform one's intellectual or political understandings of it."[21] Success, from that perspective, could be measured by the degree to which the students embraced feminism and "made commitments to political activism."[22] The creation of a "safe space" made students "very comfortable, so I could express my feelings openly."[23] Such workshops were pitched as simultaneously "nonjudgmental" and transformative, with the consequence that some students had their feelings validated and others tended to self-censor. Such classrooms were, above all, "a safe place [for students and instructors] to speak their 'feminist truths,'" which has often meant making such classrooms quite unsafe for those who might criticize or doubt those "feminist truths."[24]

From those beginnings, the advocacy for safe spaces on the university campus has proliferated. Not only individual classrooms are to be designated safe spaces, but the entire campus. Along with the expansion of the physical and temporal space to be made safe came a stretching of the dangers from which the students needed to be protected. From a space in which students can feel comfortable sharing their experiences and expressing their feelings, the focus has shifted to an "identity-safe environment" in which students can feel accepted and welcomed for who they are and feel free from the perception that they might be judged on the basis of features of their self-identity.[25] As the possible threats to a student's self-esteem multiply and grow increasingly subtle, the demands for actions to eliminate those threats grow apace. Social psychologists have been busily searching for things that might operate as identity threats, and have posited such wide-ranging threats as the presence of a racial group that shows better academic performance than your own, the presence of more men than women at a math workshop, and the presence of students from the school of an athletic rival.[26] Given the extraordinary range of environmental factors that could be taken as a threat to a student's sense of social identity, it is no surprise that the invitation to enforce a "safe space" can lead to a never-ending set of demands to increase the student's comfort.

The point is not that such effects are not real or that educators should not strive to encourage students to fully participate in their own educational experience, nor that educators should not work to reduce unnecessary sources of stress. The point is simply that the endeavor to establish safe space becomes Sisyphean when expanded to this degree. Indeed, such an expansive conception of safety can easily become zero-sum. Rather than seeking to accommodate all within a general insistence that everyone be treated with equal concern and respect, the quest to root out all possible threats to psychological well-being for some can lead to a willingness to sacrifice the well-being of others.

Worse yet, the quest for such an all-encompassing safe space is damaging to other important values. When a Muslim student feels "unsafe" when other customers seem to cast hostile glances at her at the local grocery store, when other people discuss Islamic State terrorism near her, or when professors on her campus write politically charged Facebook posts about the Middle East, her demand for "safety" cannot readily be accommodated without restricting the legitimate freedom of others. If we identify *"the problem"* facing us as being that those with whom we disagree are "smart, engaging, and influential," if *"the biggest danger"* confronting us is the possibility that a professor's writings might find readers who will "listen and absorb" and even "be influenced by his words," if we warn that faculty must "watch what they say" lest others in the community take exception to it, then we have given up on the mission of the university as a place to critically examine ideas.[27] When students at Emory University feel the need to go the university president shouting, "We are in pain!" because someone had chalked pro–Donald Trump messages on university sidewalks in the run-up to the 2016 presidential elections, a student organization feels inclined to issue a statement denouncing the act of electioneering as "cowardice" and "wrong," and the university president feels obliged to respond with words of sympathy and comfort, then the university has lost sight of its core mission of exposing students to the wide range of perspectives to be found in the world around them.[28]

We should come to an appreciation of both what the idea of a safe space has to offer and what its proper limits ought to be. If a "broader, more comprehensive notion of safety" were taken to mean the establishment of a space without the threat of imminent violence, a "contemplative, even monkish world of study," and a "free space for serious conversation," then there would be little disagreement. But when a "free space of serious conversation" is further defined as a university free from "violence, whether discursive or physical," a university free from students and scholars having to engage "with obnoxious, cruel and broken-down ideas," a university free from ideas that might be regarded as "backward or troubling," a university free from "an unregulated exchange of ideas," then the question is not merely whether such a university is "utopian" but whether such a university is still committed to seeking the truth.[29]

There is nothing wrong with students and faculty wanting to learn in an environment that is welcoming and supportive. There is nothing wrong with students and faculty wanting to avoid pointless controversies and to prioritize the valuable engagement of ideas. Indeed, there is nothing wrong with students and faculty wanting the ability to disengage from intellectual battles and seek refuge among like-minded friends and colleagues. A university dedicated to the mission of advancing and disseminating knowledge need not be a "cold, Darwinian" place or "some sort of Thunderdome" in which every moment and every conversation is a struggle for survival.[30] The call for affinity housing or a single-sex lounge should be no more troubling than the presence of a fraternity, political club, or Jewish center on campus. Such physical and metaphorical spaces can be invigorating in their own right, and allow students not only to explore new ideas in a particularly encouraging environment but also to choose to set ideas aside for a time and to emotionally recharge. It would be an emotionally exhausting environment indeed if it were not possible to break bread with other members of the community without being forced into argument.

We might distinguish between a thick version of the campus safe space and a thin version. Both are valuable and both have their place in the university, but they need to be properly situated. The thick version emphasizes comfort to community members' social identity and provides emotional support among like-minded colleagues and friends. The thin version emphasizes civility, respect, and acceptance for all members of the community. Modern American universities are unusually all-encompassing institutions. They are not just workplaces or schoolhouses. They are communities whose members not only work and learn together but also live, eat, and socialize together. There are benefits to such communities, but there is always a challenge as to how best to make them liberating rather than stifling. Making the best of it will require recognizing both the diversity and the unity of the university community.

There is both physical and figurative room on campus for those thickly safe spaces. Study rooms, lounges, dining areas, housing, clubs, and even some classes are all appropriate and available options for providing students with opportunities to let down their guard and engage with others in a spirit of complete solidarity and minimal judgment. Such spaces have sometimes been portrayed, by both their proponents and their critics, as special privileges for marginalized members of the community, but they are better understood as a universal benefit. All students on campus deserve to have a place of respite from the stresses of university life, or indeed daily life.

But that does suggest that our approach to such spaces should be evenhanded. When students call for hospitable spaces for racial minorities, religious minorities, sexual identity minorities, and women, we should recognize the value that such space can provide, while at the same time recognizing that other students can find value in such spaces as well. If it is problematic for Michigan State University to convert the women's study lounge in the student union into a common space, it is equally problematic for Harvard University to sanction students who join single-sex clubs. If we welcome George Washington University's setting aside time at campus swimming pools for women only in order to accommodate Muslim students, we should question Bowdoin College's decision to disband the evangelical Bowdoin Christian Fellowship because the club would not allow atheists to run the group.[31] Finding ways to accommodate the needs of students to sometimes be apart from the bustle of the campus at large will sometimes raise tensions and will often require compromise, but those difficulties are best negotiated if we are able to think about such demands as reflecting a universal desire rather than a special interest, if we are able to treat them all with a spirit of generous accommodation, and if we are able to accept that such spaces for nurturing thick bonds of solidarity with like-minded fellows cannot become the primary orientation of the university as a whole.

The university as a whole must be committed to fostering a campus climate that is civil, respectful, and tolerant of all. That common ground of respect and tolerance is essential so that all members of the university community can gather together and engage in their shared project of learning. The campus as a whole must be open to the great diversity of students and faculty who come to American universities, a population that hails not only from all corners of the United States but from all corners of the world. In throwing the gates of the university open to all those who wish to enter and learn, the university must demand that those entering the campus accept that invitation in the spirit in which it was given. When African American students at the Air Force Academy's preparatory school were targeted with anonymous, racial slurs, the superintendent gathered the cadets to deliver a simple message: "If you can't treat someone with dignity and respect, then you need to get out."[32] Universities are safe places for expressing often profound disagreements to the extent that they insist that members of the campus community tolerate such disagreements and recognize the right of even those very different from themselves to equally enjoy the benefits of the campus.

The university strives to shelter the campus from the "real world" so that it can be a sanctuary for the free exchange of ideas and can hear from and learn from all those who have something to contribute. The insistence on tolerance for all members of the campus community should include a tolerance for those segregated safe spaces of thick fellowship as well as those integrated safe spaces of sharp contestation and debate. The thin requirement of safety for the university as a whole must include a respect for disagreement, a tolerance for wrongheadedness, and an openness to challenge. The university as a whole is inclusive precisely in order to be open to the exploration of unsettling ideas. The university is a safe environment for the provocative and the outrageous to the degree that the members of the community generally understand that the purpose of introducing the provocation is to advance our understanding of the world and enrich the intellectual environment of the campus, and not to shut down debate or cast out some portion of the community. At British universities, atheist student groups have been repeatedly censored for satirical efforts deemed potentially offensive to religious students. If a religious student might feel some discomfort at seeing a mock-up of Michelangelo's *Creation of Adam* with the Flying Spaghetti Monster substituted in for God, or a T-shirt featuring the title characters from the comic strip *Jesus & Mo*, then university administrators have been quick to threaten to have the offending students physically removed from the premises.[33] A student leader in Britain declared that "there's a place for that discussion [of controversial topics], but the question of whether it should happen in people's homes is a difficult one." The "home" is a "safe space," free from things that the residents might find "offensive." The "home" in question, however, is the entire university campus. Defining the primary mission of the university as providing students with a "home" full of "comfort" and free from "anything controversial" strips the university of any real purpose at all.[34] Students who make such demands want to sit in a Starbucks, not learn on a college campus.

The therapeutic ethos invoked by the language of safe spaces and trigger warnings has helped make them flashpoints in the larger debate about the mission of the university and the contours of free speech within it. Where advocates of this "revolutionary" new ethos see it as a rejection of a heartless, cold, Darwinian world in favor of a more idyllic space, critics see an unrealistic and undesirable aspiration to "a place without stress."[35] The worry is that

> the "safe space" metaphor drains from classroom life every impulse toward critical reflection. It's one thing to say that students should not be laughed at for posing a question or for offering a wrong answer. It's another to say that students must never be conscious of their ignorance. It's one thing to say that students should not be belittled for a personal preference or harassed because of an unpopular opinion. It's another to say that students must never be asked why their preferences and opinions are different from those of others. It's one thing to say that students should be capable of self-revelation. It's another to say that they must always like what they see revealed.[36]

If the desire to create a safe space that can enhance an inclusive educational environment results in a tendency "to censor critical thinking," then something important will have been lost. The challenge is to "manage conflict, not prohibit it."[37]

For many, the broadening demands to make campus a safe space betray a misunderstanding of what students should expect to encounter on a college campus. The debate over the terminology itself can be a bit of a distraction, posing a false choice between inclusivity and free inquiry. Those who are welcomed to campus must also understand what occurs there. At Duke University, some incoming students objected to a summer reading assignment of a graphic novel that grappled with sexuality for fear that reading it would "compromise [our] personal Christian moral beliefs."[38] In the summer after the towers of the World Trade Center fell and US troops were sent to Afghanistan, the University of North Carolina assigned a book of commentary on the Koran as the summer reading for incoming students. The conservative Family Policy Network objected, arguing that the assignment of materials on an Islamic religious text infringed on the religious freedom of Christian students.[39] A decade earlier, faculty members were the ones who objected when a student was able to persuade a committee at Connecticut College to include an "anti-feminist" book on a summer reading list.[40] Even more disconcerting, some legislators in South Carolina threatened to cut the funding of state universities giving summer reading assignments that touched on homosexual themes. A college, in their view, "has to be reasonable and sensible to the feelings and beliefs of their students." "Their stance is 'Even if you don't want to read it, we'll shove it down your throat.'"[41] Although there are certainly debates to be had over what books are recommended for incoming students, the controversies that have arisen over such assignments have too often suggested that many incoming college students expect to be sheltered from difficult ideas rather than exposed to them, and hope to tailor their studies so as to insulate themselves from new ideas rather than to challenge themselves by grappling with them. It is this misunderstanding of the university that must be resisted if higher education is to respect its own core values.

Diversity is going to bring with it disagreement, and we should welcome those disagreements for the reasons that Mill emphasized. If we are to take seriously the injunction that a more diverse academic community is a benefit because, in part, it adds to "the diversity of perspectives that are voiced in class" and creates a "better learning environment," then we cannot expect a diversity of people and experiences to mingle on a campus without jarring, sometimes heated, and sometimes deep disagreements.[42] The AAUP report on trigger warnings emphasized that the goal of a university education "is to expose students to new ideas, have them question beliefs they have taken for granted, grapple with ethical problems they have never considered, and, more generally, expand their horizons so as to become informed and responsible democratic citizens." Such an education is expected to be "uncomfortable" in a very profound sense and filled with "difficult discussions."[43] The model of unconstrained intellectual exploration that Socrates practiced in ancient Greece and that modern universities try to implement today is often unsettling and thus resisted by those who would prefer to remain set in their ways. Students frequently find their very identities and most cherished beliefs questioned in a university environment. We should want to retain that, and students should understand what they will encounter when they enter the scholarly community. Respecting all the members of that academic community means both embracing their right to be present and to participate and taking their ideas and beliefs with the seriousness that they deserve. Respect is best demonstrated by active engagement, and inclusion is best realized by the appreciation of what unites us and by the tolerance of what divides us.

## Hate Speech

In recent years, many have argued that "hate speech" is an exception to general free speech principles. Ultimately, those advocates of a more restrictive freedom of speech would like to see a reformulation of American constitutional law, which might in fact bring American judicial doctrine closer to the constitutional principles accepted in many other countries.

More immediately, they have encouraged universities to break out on their own and adopt a more restrictive approach to what speech will be allowed or tolerated on college campuses. They have won some institutional victories and lost some legal battles, but they are no doubt shaping campus debates and influencing the college culture regarding free speech. "The idea of freedom of speech," we have been told, "does not mean a blanket permission to say anything anybody thinks." Rather, the "parameters of public speech must be continually redrawn" to exclude some speakers and some ideas from the university campus.[44]

It is commonplace to hear assertions that "hate speech" is not a protected form of free expression. Former presidential candidate and Democratic National Committee chair Howard Dean defended excluding conservative speakers from college campuses on the grounds that "hate speech is not protected by the First Amendment."[45] The mayor of Portland, Oregon, asserted the same when trying to prohibit disfavored political rallies in the city.[46] The former legal correspondent for ABC News suggested that if Americans were to "read" the Constitution, they would see that "hate speech is excluded from protection."[47] Protesters who have physically assaulted other protesters have justified their actions by declaring that hate speech is unprotected.[48] Many college students are inclined to agree.[49]

As a description of American constitutional law, this is quite wrong. The term "hate speech" itself does not refer to a legally recognized category of expression, and proponents of the view that hate speech is or should be unprotected have difficulty agreeing on what the concept is supposed to include. The category of "hate speech" is sometimes framed narrowly to focus on threats, harassment, and personal insults, but often it is framed very broadly to include arguments with unpleasant conclusions. The US Supreme Court recently emphasized that university student groups "may express any viewpoint they wish— including a discriminatory one," for the court was committed to "protect[ing] the freedom to express 'the thought that we hate.' "[50] In striking down a law banning symbols arousing anger or resentment on the basis of race, religion, or gender, the court unanimously insisted that the government could not regulate expression "based on hostility—or favoritism—towards the underlying message expressed."[51] The court has been willing to carve out a narrow category of hate speech that crosses over into being a "true threat," but has insisted that government officials must distinguish a "serious expression of an intent to commit an act of unlawful violence to a particular individual or group of individuals" or "intimidation" designed to create a reasonable "fear of bodily harm or death," which can be regulated, from mere "political hyperbole," which cannot.[52] Americans may troll and curse each other and throw out racial slurs, because ultimately "giving offense is a viewpoint" and the First Amendment allows Americans to express any viewpoint they wish.[53] Americans are not allowed to threaten each other with impunity, but they are free to express hatred toward one another.

American constitutional law has long recognized that various types of expression are not protected by the general right to free speech and free press, though the scope of those exceptions has been in steady decline for a century. Until the early twentieth century, the courts held that speech, like most other conduct, was subject to myriad restrictions. As the US Supreme Court explained when upholding a conviction of a Communist Labor Party organizer in 1927, "the freedom of speech which is secured by the Constitution does not confer an absolute right to speak, without responsibility, whatever one may choose, or an unrestricted and unbridled license giving immunity for every possible use of language and preventing the punishment of those who abuse this freedom; and . . . a State in the exercise of its police powers may punish those who abuse this freedom by utterances inimical to the public welfare, tending to incite to crime, disturb the public peace, or endanger the foundations of organized government."[54] Howard Dean would have been right if he had said a hundred years ago that "hate speech is not free speech," and political majorities and government officials routinely used the power of the state to punish anyone who wrote or said things that *they* found particularly hateful. At the dawn of the twentieth century, arrests for disturbing the peace did indeed follow Prohibition activist Carrie Nation wherever she went across the country, precisely because the police regularly arrested *her* whenever "she became boisterous."[55] When the wives of striking Pennsylvania mine workers yelled at those crossing the picket line and called them "scabs" in 1903, the women were likewise arrested for disturbing the peace.[56] Whether such "hate speech" was to be punished was a matter of political discretion. Progressives scored a great victory when this constitutional standard was abandoned and the court began a steady march toward extending constitutional protection to a wide range of political dissenters, social activists, religious agitators, and artists (not to mention the occasional pornographer).

The old constitutional standard that judges enforced over the course of the nineteenth century fairly easily accommodated laws regulating hate speech. Government officials and the police were often enthusiastic about shutting down speech that they found offensive, hateful, or dangerous. On the eve of World War II, for example, the police in Rochester, New Hampshire, were quick to whisk away Walter Chaplinsky, who

had riled up a crowd on a public sidewalk with his proselytiza-
tion for the Jehovah's Witnesses and his condemnation of
Catholics. When Chaplinsky then told the police officers that
they were "damned Fascists" for suppressing his sidewalk
preaching, they promptly arrested him and charged him with
the crime of calling someone an "offensive or derisive name"
and acting so as to "deride, offend or annoy." At that point in
its history, the court was willing to allow the state to prosecute
someone for "insulting or 'fighting' words—those which by
their very utterance inflict injury or tend to incite an immediate breach of the peace." As the justices observed, "such utterances are no essential part of any exposition of ideas, and are
of such slight social value as a step to truth that any benefit that
may be derived from them is clearly outweighed by the social
interest in order and morality."[57]

Within just a few years, the court was having second
thoughts. Not long after the end of the war, the disgraced Catholic priest Arthur Terminiello was arrested for disturbing the
peace at a raucous public meeting in Chicago. Terminiello was
a controversial figure—a fierce critic of President Franklin
Roosevelt, an opponent of American entry into the war, a pro-
ponent of anti-Semitic conspiracy theories—and his speech
attracted a "surging, howling mob" of protesters who broke
windows, threw bottles, and assaulted police officers guarding
the meeting room. In upholding his conviction for inciting a
riot, the state court concluded that Terminiello was a "professional agitator" who was making "an appeal to fury" by baiting
what he termed the "slimy scum" and "skunks of Jews" who
protested his talk.[58] The US Supreme Court reversed that conviction as unconstitutional, asserting that "a function of free
speech under our system of government is to invite dispute,"
stir "people to anger," and "have profound unsettling effects as

it presses for acceptance of an idea."[59] The justices did not question whether Terminiello's words were hurtful or enraging, but they insisted that every citizen had a duty to refrain from violence regardless of such provocations. Those guilty of disturbing the peace were the ones breaking windows and throwing punches, not those giving speeches. The court has charted a liberalizing course on free speech ever since, emphasizing that the state cannot silence or punish citizens because their words or actions were offensive, generated raw emotions, were abusive to particular groups, or advocated policies that the government or popular majorities thought positively evil.

When American colleges began to adopt new policies regulating "hate speech" on campus in the 1980s, they ran into legal objections based on the court's interpretation of the First Amendment. Unsurprisingly, the college administrators who initiated and drafted the new policies were less concerned about protecting free speech than with avoiding the bad publicity that might come from a racially charged incident on campus. The claim generally was that such policies were not "speech codes" at all and did not restrict the expression of ideas, but were instead codes of "civility" that aimed only at deterring "bad behavior."[60] Meanwhile, an emerging generation of legal activists began to build arguments that hate speech should not be protected by the US Constitution. "Racist speech is best treated as a *sui generis* category," one that is "so tied to violence and degradation" that it should be uniquely subject to prohibition.[61] Hate speech should be regarded as a form of "discursive violence" rather than a form of expression.[62] Judges have not yet been persuaded.

The shifting decisions of the US Supreme Court have immediate consequences for state universities, but they can also help illuminate the broader issues that ought to be of interest to anyone thinking about the appropriate principles of free speech on a college campus. It is first worth setting aside some potential rationales for protecting hate speech before considering why a hate speech exception might still not be the best course of action.

First, the resistance to a specific hate speech exception to the general commitment to free speech need not suggest that such speech is harmless. The traditional regulation of all kinds of speech was based on the assumption that speech could be dangerous, hurtful, and damaging, and that the state was empowered to suppress anything that was harmful, including speech. The civil libertarians who argued for greater protection for speech did not contend that such speech is really harmless. They argued that speech should be protected *even though* it is harmful. Critics of campus speech codes often invoke the familiar rhyme "Sticks and stones may break my bones, but words will never hurt me," but this is rarely persuasive. Both the crying child and the comforting parent know that words do in fact hurt. The rhyme is not meant to be descriptive; it is meant to be aspirational. The parent does not deny the pain, but rather urges the child to overcome the pain and not let those emotional wounds define her. Similarly, advocates of free speech should not deny the harm that can be caused by words or dismiss the reality that speech can be dangerous. While metaphorical flights of fancy (such as the rhetoric of "discursive violence") can attribute to hate speech a potency that seems unwarranted, we should be cautious not to lean too far the other way and assert that the harm caused by hate speech is fanciful.

We should pause for a moment to acknowledge the role that metaphors have played in the rhetoric of hate speech. It is now routine for words to be characterized as doing "violence" to the listener, or even to those far removed from the speech. The social theorist Michel Foucault argued that there was "violence" inherent in speech and ideas because we use them to impose our will upon the world around us.[63] It has become fashionable in some circles to talk of the sin of "intellectual violence," which can include, for example, holding a negative view of the left-wing philosopher Jacques Derrida without having thoroughly read his oeuvre.[64] From a different angle, the sociologist Patricia Hill Collins has emphasized that there is a "symbiotic relationship linking actions and speech," between "racist and sexist ideas [and] violence." This is no doubt true, but it obscures more than it illuminates to collapse the difference between speech and action and to simply refer to "verbal violence."[65]

Once words are taken to be equivalent to violence, then the call for censorship quickly follows. It should be no surprise that the rhetoric of discursive violence has proliferated and been embraced by all sides. Thus a student has argued that since "words are actions," the difference between "a racist pamphlet" and murder "can be only of degree."[66] A professor at the University of Illinois derided the chancellor of the university because her call for "civility" on campus should be understood as "a prime example of violent language—all the more violent because of its calm, rational, removed tone."[67] Gay rights activists denounce street preachers as engaging in "verbal violence."[68] An education theorist asserts that those who criticize campus activists are engaged in "intellectual violence."[69] Exposing a sociologist's plagiarism is "a form of intellectual violence wrapped in objective scholarship."[70] A psychologist calls out her brethren in the African American community for committing "heinous act[s] of violence against one another" by the "use of unloving and unsafe language."[71]

Donald Trump's presidential campaign is described as "endless acts of public verbal violence" that "numbs people's senses to the point that they no longer fully register the horror of what they are living through."[72] When a conservative student group was chastised for engaging in offensive satire, it responded by denouncing its critics for their "violent and hateful rhetoric."[73] A white Canadian artist's paintings are removed from a gallery because she is engaged in "cultural genocide" by painting in the style of a famed Indigenous artist.[74] Such rhetorical turns of phrase are certainly vivid and for some purposes might even be useful. These metaphors would be worthy of little notice if not for the fact that they are now used as justifications for censorship. If we elide the real distinctions between speech and actual physical violence, however, we open the door not only to widespread censorship of disfavored ideas but to the use of actual violence against unpopular speakers in the name of "self-defense." The suggestion that speakers should be suppressed if their words might inspire, encourage, justify, or contribute to acts of physical violence would lead as easily to the censorship of socialist icon Emma Goldman or civil rights leader Malcolm X as to that of current right-wing writers Ann Coulter or Milo Yiannopoulos. We significantly shrink the scope of political and social debate if we conflate the proper effort to punish and deter acts of physical violence and the more dubious effort to suppress speech that might potentially lead to violence.

Second, hate speech need not be regarded as particularly valuable. It is an easy temptation to exclude some forms of expression from the realm of protected speech by deeming such categories of speech to be literally worthless. Some of the justices on the US Supreme Court, for example, have suggested that books could be banned only if they were "utterly without redeeming social value,"[75] or words could be punished only when they are "by definition worthless and undeserving of constitutional protection."[76] One legal scholar has described this as a "two-level theory" of free speech in which some speech is "worthy enough" to deserve protection while other speech is "apparently so worthless" that it can be banned completely.[77] Such a test has invited efforts to argue that almost any speech has some sort of value, even if it is only primarily valuable to the speaker. These efforts are often rather strained and generally come down to a claim that such speech is a form of authentic self-expression. As society has become more tolerant of diversity, dissent, and the unconventional, judges have become less willing to toss aside outrageous forms of expression as wholly without value. "One man's vulgarity is another's lyric."[78]

The more immediate question for universities is whether such speech contributes to the mission of a university, and for that purpose the value of hate speech (at least as narrowly defined) seems quite limited. Universities are committed to the search for truth, and the value of speech to a community of scholars lies in whether it can help us advance or communicate knowledge. Speech can be expressive without being particularly productive. The liberal tradition of tolerating dissent, approaching offensive ideas with an open mind, and treating one's own convictions with a healthy dose of skepticism gives no reason for seeking out hate speech. Free scholarly inquiry and the rigorous testing of ideas are not likely to suffer if personal invectives or racial slurs are excluded from campus. Hate speech of that limited sort is not a valuable component of the academic enterprise.

If hate speech is neither harmless nor valuable, then why should it be tolerated? Or, more to the point, why would the principles of free speech that ought to guide a campus community counsel caution in suppressing hate speech? Here we should recall the Jeffersonian lessons regarding speech restrictions. In the years after the American Revolution, many in the founding generation thought that it was both essential and possible to suppress bad speech in order to protect the republic. They soon discovered that it was an impossible task to preserve freedom and censor speech. Once an official has been empowered to suppress speech, it is inevitable that good speech will be suppressed along with the bad, that the tools forged to punish worthless speech will be used to silence valuable speech as well.

The idea that a hate speech exception would be applied strictly and stay limited flies in the face of our historical experience. When charged with the duty to suppress harmful speech, officials have repeatedly understood that duty as a mandate to suppress unpopular speech and speech that they personally find offensive and unpalatable. When Puritan leaders claimed the right to suppress false and dangerous speech, they drove religious dissenters into the wilderness. When the Federalists empowered judges to suppress false and dangerous speech, those Federalist judges promptly jailed Jeffersonian newspaper editors. When slave owners claimed the right to suppress false and dangerous speech, they burned abolitionist publishers to the ground. When the legal establishment embraced the right to suppress false and dangerous speech at the turn of the twentieth century, they jailed socialists and anarchists. When university administrators have been asked to suppress speech harmful to the campus community, they have been as likely to prohibit civil rights activists and Communist professors as white supremacists. The gradual loosening of the bonds of censorship in the United States over the past century has come about through the repeated recognition that exceptions to free speech are exploited by those in power to suppress speech that they find threatening. Civil libertarians have responded not by insisting on an absolute right to free speech but by eliminating and narrowing exceptions to free speech as much as possible.

We need not turn to the broader history of censorship of harmful speech to see how exceptions, once created, are expanded to suit the immediate interests of those exercising power. The brief history of hate speech policies has already provided evidence in abundance of that same dynamic.

The adoption of university speech codes quickly led to litigation, which in turn revealed the extent to which such policies were overly broad in the speech and conduct that they attempted to suppress, and often arbitrary in how they were enforced. The very category of "hate speech" has no clear definition and no obvious boundaries. The University of Michigan, for example, swept up in its student conduct policy not only express or implied threats directed to other students but also any speech that "stigmatizes or victimizes an individual" on the basis of a long list of characteristics. The university's own guidelines for how the policy was to be enforced gave examples that ranged from racist threats to neglecting to invite a student to a party or arguing in class that "women just aren't as good in this field as men." In practice, a social work student was disciplined for arguing in class for the benefits of conversion therapy for homosexuals, and a dentistry student was disciplined for complaining to another student that he had heard that minority students were treated unfairly in a particular class. Reviewing the record, a federal judge determined that Michigan's policy indiscriminately encompassed both constitutionally protected speech and unprotected threats, and employed language so vague that it "was simply impossible to discern any limitation on its scope or any conceptual distinction between protected and unprotected conduct."[79] Courts reviewing policies at other colleges and universities reached similar conclusions. In an effort to draft policies that were flexible enough to cover all possible incidents that might arise on campus, college administrators tended to adopt rules that gave them great discretion to punish all sorts of speech and gave students little guidance as to how to avoid charges being filed against them. Rather than adopting narrow policies that targeted true threats, college administrators regularly favored policies that prohibited anything they found demeaning or offensive. Rather than restricting themselves to intervening in student affairs when someone had been threatened with violence, college administrators routinely policed the tone and content of student arguments and even classroom discussions. Rather than relying on faculty to teach and correct students who made weak or misguided but inflammatory arguments, they authorized administrators to discipline those students.

One approach to trying to confine the scope of hate speech regulations is to argue that racist speech is uniquely threatening. A prominent advocate of campus hate speech regulation, Mari Matsuda, early on contended that "in order to respect first amendment values, a narrow definition of actionable racist speech is required. Racist speech is best treated as a *sui generis* category." Racist speech should be treated as "qualitatively different" from all other speech, and as a result uniquely subject to regulation and prohibition.[80] In practice, however, hate speech codes have never been limited in that way. The University of Michigan policy, for example, listed no fewer than twelve distinct categories of victimization that were subject to special protection, including speech that was thought to demean someone based on age, marital status, or Vietnam-era veteran status. A hate-speech policy at the University of

Wisconsin, struck down as unconstitutional not long after the Michigan policy, punished speech that demeaned individuals on the basis of ten possible categories. In keeping with a more recent wave of policymaking, the private Dickinson College adopted a "bias incident protocol" to "respond to an expression that may be offensive or inflammatory to some," regardless of "whether the act or expression was intentional or unintentional," and that might give offense "based on but not limited to" a list of ten protected categories.[81] Speech that unintentionally gives offense to someone on the basis of a characteristic not previously identified by school policy can make a student subject to administrative actions by campus officials.

The ongoing development and implementation of such policies—in some cases even after they have been struck down as unconstitutional—lends no support to the hope that racist speech might be treated as unique. Instead, concerns about racist speech have been treated as an opening wedge for far more wide-ranging policies designed to empower college officials to police campus speech that some might regard as offensive. Such policies have been embraced to an even greater degree outside the United States. King's College London, for example, requires that outside speakers have the text of their speech vetted by campus officials before it can be delivered, and University College London prohibits speech that might be regarded as "offensive or provocative."[82] University College London banned the Nietzsche Club because the German philosopher was also admired by associates of Adolf Hitler.[83] The London School of Economics found itself backpedaling after students in an atheist club were harassed by school officials for wearing T-shirts with a cartoon image of Muhammad, but such efforts to censor religious images that "may cause distress and insult to others" have been a frequent point of contention on British campuses.[84] A Scottish university student association banned a pro-life group because the "students largely do not want anything to do with a group that promotes the removal of rights over bodily autonomy for over half the student population that attend this university."[85]

One might at least hope that the regulation of hate speech could be narrowly tailored so as to just restrict such low-value utterances as slurs, obscenities, and invectives aimed at particular individuals (though that too would raise constitutional problems), but from its beginnings the movement to regulate hate speech was aimed at the suppression of disfavored arguments and ideas. That was certainly true in practice, as when Michigan disciplined the social work student for a classroom argument in favor of conversion therapy, but it was embedded in the theory of hate speech regulation as well. When Matsuda argued that racist speech should be treated as uniquely deserving of censorship, the claim was not limited to racial slurs but was directed explicitly to "racist messages." On this view, political and social ideas should be suppressed once they pass some threshold of having been "collectively and internationally considered and rejected."[86] The argument for restricting hate speech rests on the claim that some ideas are simply more deserving than others, and thus only some ideas are worthy of being heard. By their nature, the authorities empowered to determine what ideas are worthy of being heard are not faculty members teaching their classes or advancing their scholarship, but campus administrators imposing sanctions on members of the campus community. Messages that "further justice, equality, and social contentment" should be heard. Messages that work against social justice should be suppressed. Speech should be suppressed not when it incites violence but when it "elicit[s] fears about historical outgroups" and promotes ideologies that we would prefer not to see prevail.[87] Some ideas should be designated by university administrators as "false," and those holding such ideas should not merely be educated by faculty engaging with them; they are to be censored so that they may not speak those ideas.[88]

Unsurprisingly, the argument that hate speech should not be tolerated on college campuses has been used not merely to discipline students who use a racial slur during a heated argument or leave threatening messages on a dorm room door. It has been used to justify shutting down campus speakers who want to advocate for Donald Trump, contend that immigration should be restricted, criticize the Black Lives Matter movement and its policy proposals, argue against progressive sexual mores, or posit that those accused of sexual assault on campus should be given a fair hearing. Such expansive applications of the hate speech exception to free speech are the natural and predictable result of adopting the view that only politically desirable speech should be protected. Anything that does not further justice, as conceived and understood by college administrators, should be classified as hate speech and suppressed. The logic of restricting exposure to such hateful speech does not suggest a stopping point with speakers. If students should not be exposed to Ann Coulter or Charles Murray in a campus auditorium, there seems to be no more reason why they should be exposed to their books in the library or permitted to access their work on campus computer networks. If "keeping watch over the soul of our republic" means "redefining the rules of what counts as public speech," then some ideas will be labeled as simply too dangerous to be allowed onto a college campus.[89] Universities will be distinguished not by their willingness to boldly explore new ideas and subject conventional wisdom to close scrutiny, but by their unwillingness to grapple with the very ideas that occupy the public sphere, and that can be found at the corner bookstore or on the cable news show.

College campuses do have an alternative that addresses the core concern of hate speech regulations while preserving a robust commitment to free speech. The label of "hate speech" has always covered a vague and disparate set of offenses, opening the door to selective and abusive enforcement against controversial speakers and ideas at the whim of campus officials. The defensible kernel of the hate speech exception, however, is limited to personal threats and harassment. Campus administrators have a responsibility to secure a safe environment for students to learn, and thus a responsibility to discipline those who seek, for any reason, to harass or threaten members of the campus community. Instructors leading a classroom discussion have a duty to correct students who make baseless or misguided arguments. The very goal of instruction and research is to expose flawed arguments for what they are. Part of the process of teaching students is to guide them in how to develop and state arguments so that ideas can be constructively considered and ill-considered expressions of opinion or emotional outbursts can be minimized.

The faculty members and staff of a university have an obligation to socialize and train students to engage in civil but passionate debate about important, controversial, and sometimes offensive subjects, and to be able to critically examine arguments and ideas that they find attractive as well as those they find repulsive. Colleges and universities will have failed in their educational mission if they produce graduates who are incapable of facing up to and judiciously engaging difficult ideas. Preparing students for a lifetime of responsible citizenship and enabling the campus community to fearlessly investigate the strength of competing ideas requires cultivating not an environment in which students and scholars are sheltered from disreputable ideas, but one in which those ideas can be respectfully and forcefully confronted. Arguments and ideas that some might find hateful might well be deeply flawed and widely rejected. We gain the most for good ideas, however, if we demonstrate why bad ideas are mistaken rather than treat them as taboo. Moreover, even in vanquishing bad ideas, we may strengthen and improve our own. In an institution of teaching and learning, we expect students to learn how to identify flawed arguments and set aside bad ideas rather than simply be told that some conclusions should be taken on faith and some ideas are too dangerous and enticing to be contemplated. We advance truth not by burning the books of the wicked but by winning converts through the force of persuasion.

## Forms of Protest

There are many calls to restrict free speech on college campuses in the name of other values, but sometimes the impairment of free speech comes dressed as the expansion of free speech. Some have suggested that "when you simply have two people talking at once, civil libertarians don't necessarily have a clear way to choose between them."[90] This is simply wrong. Although it should rarely be the case that the exercise of free speech by some actually interferes with the exercise of free speech by others, it should be recognized that free speech can thrive only under conditions of appropriate regulation. The best environment for the productive exchange of ideas is not the mosh pit. Anytime there are large groups of people with something to say, some orderly procedures need to be put in place if individuals are going to be able to make themselves heard and an actual collective conversation can take place.

Classroom discussions are managed by an instructor. Faculty meetings follow Robert's Rules of Order. Similarly, vigorous debate in the campus equivalent of the public square requires some ground rules.

The US Supreme Court has long adhered to a useful framework for thinking about how government regulations that affect speech should be viewed under the First Amendment of the US Constitution. The court is particularly open to so-called time, place, and manner regulations that try to channel free speech in productive ways and coordinate the many activities in which citizens are engaged in the shared public space, while being much more skeptical of regulations that restrict the content of speech or unnecessarily limit the ability of a speaker to reach an audience. This is not merely a matter of preventing governmental suppression of speech, or imposing a social order that tolerates only those who "speak decorously." This is a matter of maintaining social spaces that allow for both vigorous protest and critical dialogue, that allow for both the expression of grievances and argumentation, that allow for both inclusive participation and the productive exchange of ideas. Such principles aim for the realization of a freedom of speech that does not depend on the forbearance of either the mob or the censor.

Bearing such a distinction in mind is useful for thinking about forms of protest as well, and for thinking about when appropriate expressions of dissent cross a line and become damaging to the ability of others to enjoy their own freedoms in the campus community. Thinking through how best to manage the vigorous exchange of ideas by passionate advocates is important in part because we should recognize the value of protest and dissent. Over the past several decades, the story of the development of constitutional law in this area has to a significant degree been the story of expanding protections for a widening array of protest activities. Our constitutional law has recognized that in order to effectively exercise their right to free speech, dissenters must be able to choose not only their message but its form of delivery. Dissenters need the freedom to grab the attention of the public, to dramatize their concerns, and to convey their message in a way that makes sense and is accessible to both themselves and their intended audience. The growing appreciation for that basic principle has led judges to push government officials to accommodate the expression of dissent, whether that dissent takes the form of a march or a demonstration, a sit-in or a silent vigil, a stump speech or a burning flag, a reasoned argument or a passionate obscenity. The starting point for an appreciation of the value of free speech on campus should be an appreciation of the many forms of protest and the need to make space for them.

Protests can be invigorating and rousing to an audience, but they can also be discomforting and intimidating. Here too we must remind ourselves that discomfort is to be expected and does not in itself provide a reason for shutting down dissent. A group of students at Princeton University made the point clearly when defending some of their own protest activities. Along with students at many universities across the United States in the fall of 2015, a group known as the Black Justice League mounted increasingly visible demonstrations calling for a wide variety of changes on the Princeton campus. The protests at Princeton, as on many other campuses, were often enthusiastic and turbulent and were designed to maximize the attention to their particular cause. Some observers reacted rather critically, complaining about both tone and tactics. Setting aside for the moment the details of those tactics, I want to call attention to a general point made by the Black

Justice League in responding to those complaints. They dismissed such complaints as "an attempt to tone-police and silence those whose voices have historically been repressed." While it no doubt goes too far to say that the call for "civil discourse" is necessarily an attempt to "silence" the repressed, the underlying point is an important one. It is stifling to dissent to insist that the dissenters "present their concerns in a way that is most palatable to those who are responsible for addressing their grievances." The students were particularly concerned that such a rhetorical move had the effect of "placing the burden back on those marginalized to prove themselves worthy of being heard."[91] They correctly rejected the implication that dissenters have an obligation to approach others with hat in hand and in a tone of submission, or that some students were not due the respect of a hearing unless they adopted the manner of speech favored by others. We each have the right to determine not only what we want to say but also how we say it, and we must always be open to engaging with those who choose to express themselves differently than we would ourselves.

The demand for respect is, however, a two-way street. Demands for "civility" and "good order" can become tools to censor and suppress, but they are also important values in society in general and in a university in particular. We should strive to address each other with civility, and we should recognize that passion can often get in the way of reason. The ultimate goal of a university community is to foster an environment in which competing perspectives can be laid bare, heard, and assessed. Recognizing the equal dignity of each member of the community entails a willingness to listen, but also a willingness to engage in dialogue. We should all strive to be charitable and generous in tolerating those occasions when passion gets the better of us and our words are not chosen as carefully as they should have been. It is inevitable that when ideas are taken seriously and held with conviction, they will sometimes be expressed strongly, and even too strongly. Just as the listener should strive to be forgiving when the speaker oversteps the bounds of civility, so the speaker should strive to be diligent in observing the bounds of civility and trying to stay within them. Being uncivil does not make one unworthy of being heard, but it might make one less likely to be listened to. We try to be civil to each other not because we need to demonstrate that we are worthy of being heard, but because civility breeds dialogue, mutual respect, and ultimately the productive exchange of ideas.

Mill's search for the truth advances not through shouting matches, but through reasoned deliberation. He wanted all sides to be able to make their best arguments with conviction, but the entire point of the exercise is to make the arguments available for others to evaluate. The members of the university community have the right to have their arguments heard. They have the right to expect that others in the community will be open to persuasion. They do not have the right to insist that others in fact find the arguments persuasive, nor to expel from the community those who disagree. Respecting each member of the community requires respecting the right of each to be present and to make up his or her own mind.

The marketplace of ideas is crowded. One challenge of participating in that marketplace is simply to gain attention. One point of protest activities is to try to increase the chance of being heard, to demand attention. Universities provide myriad venues through which the exchange of ideas can occur, from classrooms to academic journals, from conferences to public meetings, from newspapers to flyers, from the Internet to social media. Protests are designed to cut through the clutter and draw an immediate audience to hear the protester's chosen message. Universities should make space for that as well and allow dissenters to get their message out as best they can, so long as they do not unduly interfere with the ability of others to pursue their own separate goals on the shared campus.

Let us recall that the purpose and value of free speech within a university is its truth-seeking function. The free exchange of ideas, spirited argumentation, and careful evaluation of those arguments all contribute to the university's mission of advancing and disseminating knowledge. Protests can further that process by calling attention to a neglected set of concerns and ideas. Once you have my attention, however, what are you going to do with it? The protester has a responsibility to transition from actions geared primarily toward gaining publicity to the development and articulation of arguments to be evaluated by the assembled community of scholars. If protests never make that turn, if they never get to the point of entering into reasoned debate, then they contribute little to the intellectual life and ultimate mission of a university.

The energetic effort to get attention for one's cause can be taken too far. Here I want to consider two closely related types of difficulties that are frequently encountered and the principles that should help guide us in identifying the boundaries of appropriate protest activities on campus. The first we might characterize as the problem of disruption, and the second we might characterize as obstruction or the classic problem of the "heckler's veto." In both cases, the activity of protesting no longer serves as an adjunct to the free exchange of ideas. Rather than fostering debate, disruption and obstruction make the exchange of ideas more difficult. Rather than pursuing the goal of persuasion through reasoned argument, disruption and obstruction seek simply to coerce in order to win compliance.

There is no contribution to advancing knowledge; there is only an effort to compel others to obey.

Disruption takes many forms, but they all aim to impede the normal functioning of the university. A poster hung by the activist group By Any Means Necessary (BAMN) at the University of California at Berkeley is exemplary of the tactic. In 1996, the voters of the state of California approved Proposition 209, which prohibited public institutions from discriminating on the basis of race. Most immediately, it banned certain forms of affirmative action in state universities. BAMN mobilized to protest the adoption and implementation of Prop 209 on the Berkeley campus, declaring,

> We must force Chancellor Tien to publicly state that the Berkeley campus will defy 209! We must continue and expand the mass actions such as the Campanile occupation and marches through buildings on campus. We must demonstrate that the campus will be ungovernable unless Tien accept our demands.[92]

Mass action, direct action, occupation, sit-in, disruption, civil disobedience. They have all become commonplace tactics on college campuses. So common, in fact, that we should introduce a distinction between actual disruptions and what we might call staged disruptions.

Many protest activities are designed less to be a disruption than to give the appearance of disruption. They create temporary impediments that are soon cleared away so that normal activity can resume. The point of such a tactic is not so much to disrupt as to call attention to the cause. Frequently the ground rules for these sorts of protests are carefully negotiated among campus administrators, campus security, and the protesting students. The staging of the disruption itself is a Kabuki theater of choreographed moves by which the protesters are allowed to make their point and everyone else is able to continue their activities after a brief interruption. Such staged disruptions can simply be built in to ordinary event planning, with everyone understanding that the scheduled speaker, for example, will actually begin a few minutes later than what is announced in the program, or that the individual heckler will soon be ushered from the auditorium so that a presentation can continue unimpeded for those who wish to see it.

Unfortunately, it is sometimes hard for administrators to know whether a given protest is intended to be an actual disruption or a staged disruption, and such misunderstandings can create unnecessary tensions. In the fall of 2015, one group of demonstrators marched in the Homecoming Parade at the University of Missouri with signs declaring their support for minority students at the university. A second group of demonstrators, calling themselves Concerned Student 1950, chose to occupy the parade route and block the car carrying the University of Missouri system president Tim Wolfe. Since the demonstration was not coordinated ahead of time, it was not immediately clear whether the protesters would soon move out of the way or would instead try to continue to disrupt the parade. As one supporter of Concerned Student 1950 later explained, "They have to do something to be noticed."[93] From that perspective, the blockade was a staged disruption, and as it happens the protesters soon dispersed after a fifteen-minute delay of the parade. In the meantime, however, the uncertainty as to what was happening led to some unnecessary pushing and shoving. From the perspective of the goals of free speech on campus, there is nothing wrong with staged disruptions. They are simply another device for calling attention to a particular cause, for getting noticed.

Actual disruptions are different. They are not designed to be temporary events to attract attention. They are rather designed to make the university, as BAMN put it, "ungovernable." They are intended to "force" university officials to comply with a set of "demands" if the disruption is to come to an end and the university is to return to normal. In effect, protesters engaged in actual disruption seek to take other members of the campus hostage, demanding concessions in exchange for their freedom.

This is the language of coercion, not persuasion. Indeed, such tactics are often justified precisely because efforts at persuasion seem to have failed. Other members of the campus community either refuse to pay sufficient attention to protesters' favored cause, or they refuse to come to the conclusion that the protesters desire. But, of course, in a free and equal community of scholars, all individuals are at liberty to focus their attention on the issues of greatest concern to them and to reach conclusions about those issues that make the most sense to them. The advancement of knowledge comes through the testing of ideas and the drawing of conclusions about their merits, not through the forced acceptance of ideas. Forced compliance with favored doctrine is precisely what the liberal tradition was born rejecting, and the modern university is premised on the belief that such indoctrination is inconsistent with the pursuit of truth and greater understanding of the world in which we live. Disruptive actions designed to prevent other members of the community from pursuing the basic mission of the university and to force compliance with a set of demands are antithetical to the very purpose of a university. This is no longer the exercise of free speech, but the opposite.

Efforts aimed at impeding the normal rhythm of university life subvert rather than realize the mission of a university.

There are, of course, degrees of disruption, and some are more tolerable than others. Prudent toleration should not be confused with principled endorsement, however. In the spring of 2016, the members of a student group called Reclaim Harvard Law occupied a lounge in the student center at the Harvard Law School. The students christened the lounge "Belinda Hall" in honor of a slave held by one of the early benefactors of the law school, and issued a list of demands for improving race relations in the law school. During the course of the occupation, the protesting students argued both that they were taking direct action to create a "safe space" for minority students within the law school and that they were engaging in an occupation of part of a university building with a list of demands to be satisfied before they would vacate.[94] In that case, university officials decided to accommodate the occupation, eventually insisting only that the students allow the room to be cleaned and not engage in violent confrontations with other students. Although the activists eventually began to openly ponder "redrawing our lines" and occupying more of the law school since their demands were not being met to their satisfaction, the school's decision to tolerate the occupation was ultimately a prudential calculation that the disruption caused by use of one room within the student center did not impede the general operation of the law school and the ability of faculty and students to engage in their primary pursuits. By contrast, when a coalition of several groups of students at Ohio State University occupied the central administration building during that same spring because they were frustrated that university officials had not acted on their various demands, the university promptly warned the students that they would be arrested and expelled from the university if they did not end the occupation within hours of its start. The students quickly vacated the premises.[95] At both Ohio State and Harvard, the disruption was in clear violation of university policies and student codes of conduct. The question of whether to enforce those rules became a prudential one about which officials might differ depending on the particular circumstances. But in neither case was there a question of student free speech. Although both groups of students integrated some argumentative efforts into their protests (teach-ins at Harvard, an open mic at Ohio State), the primary purpose of the activity was to disrupt the lives of other members of the university community and force compliance with the activists' own objectives. The ability of the campus community to pursue its central mission was impeded rather than advanced by their efforts. The decision to put an end to the disruption ultimately works to uphold the conditions for the free exchange of ideas at the university.

This is not to say that such occupations and mass actions may not be justifiable. If they are justified, however, it is not because the activists are engaged in the exercise of free speech in pursuit of the truth-seeking mission of the university. Rather they would have to be justified as appropriate instances of civil disobedience. In this spirit, the students in Princeton's Black Justice League invoked the example of Martin Luther King Jr. and the history of civil disobedience in order to bring about justice. As they observed, there are certainly conditions of injustice that would justify the disruption of the civil order. But note that this is no longer a claim about the university as such, the free exchange of ideas, or the goal of advancing knowledge. The protesters are not taking action as students or as members of a scholarly community. They are taking political action as concerned citizens seeking redress for societal wrongs. In responding to critics of his tactics of "non-violent direct action," King posited that there were circumstances that justified breaking "an unjust law" but one "must do so openly, lovingly, and with a willingness to accept the penalty." If the situation is dire enough, students might risk expulsion "in order to arouse the conscience of the community," but presumably such situations should be rare.[96] Given their concerns, the students in Berkeley's BAMN could have mounted their disruptive protest of the new state constitutional amendment anywhere, from the state capitol building to the local firehouse, and it was mere happenstance that BAMN's membership included some students. The university was simply a convenient, and perhaps unusually tolerant, site for trying to affect state politics.

The claim of such disruptive protests is not that the participants are engaged in a debate in order to seek the truth about social justice. The claim is that they already know the truth about social justice. The disruptive protest is an effort to implement that knowledge, not to critically examine it or offer it to others for their critical examination. In doing so, they echo the famed declaration of 1960s Berkeley student leader Mario Savio, who called upon activists not to engage in a debate but to simply impede. "There is a time," he said, "when the operation of the machine becomes so odious, makes you so sick at heart, that you can't take part. . . . You've got to put your bodies upon the gears and upon the wheels, the levers, upon all the apparatus, and you've got to make it stop."[97] When the time for action has arrived, the time for talking has come to an end. The question to be asked about any given disruptive protest is whether the disruption to social order is justified from the general perspective of a liberal democratic society, not whether the protest falls within the ambit of the free speech that is essential to the mission of a university. Perhaps the act of coercion is justifiable as part of the process of bringing about justice, but it is not an example of free speech or behavior designed to advance the pursuit of truth. Perhaps universities should be forgiving of such coercive tactics on their campuses, but forbearance in the face of the disruption of campus activities is hard to justify if the injustice being protested is not grave and the disturbance is not slight. Administrators might be patient with students occupying a student lounge or study room, but unforgiving with students occupying a classroom or an administrative office.

The second and related form of protest activity is obstruction. In the case of disruption, the goal is to impede university life and to impose costs on members of the community in the hopes that they will concede to demands in order to alleviate the pressure. In the case of obstruction, the goal is more particular. Obstruction is intended to prevent disfavored speech from taking place or from being heard. There is no broader set of demands to be met. The "injustice" to be prevented is the speech being obstructed. If that is accomplished, then the obstruction is successful. Obstructions are about enforcing limits on the ideas that can be peacefully communicated on campus and shrinking the scope of intellectual inquiry. Disruption is a means to an end, but obstruction is the end to be achieved in itself.

Obstruction can take myriad forms, some posing more serious threats to the intellectual life on campus than others, but all working against free speech and open inquiry. Just as the means for the communication of ideas on campus are various, so too are the means for obstructing communication varied. During the Reclaim Harvard Law occupation of the student center lounge, students on each side of the dispute vandalized and destroyed each other's posters. Signs announcing events and publications left in newsstands on campus are easy targets and are often destroyed by those who object to the message being communicated. The physical space hosting a speech or a conference can be occupied and disrupted to such a degree that opponents are prevented from speaking. The examples of such obstructions are numerous. Infamously, at Middlebury College in the spring of 2017, activists occupied the auditorium in which the conservative social scientist Charles Murray was to speak. Their mere presence displaced interested listeners who were not able to join the audience to hear the talk. If protesters occupy every seat or almost every seat of a venue but then stand in silent protest of the speech, they are still obstructing the speech by preventing those who actually want to listen to it from being able to occupy those seats. At Middlebury, however, the students were not content with a silent protest. Instead, they engaged in a lengthy round of chanting, singing, clapping, and shouting so that it was impossible to speak over them, and in such large numbers that it was not easy to remove them. Eventually university officials gave up, canceled the lecture, and moved Murray to another room to engage in a webcast conversation with a member of the faculty. The protesters followed Murray to the new building, making noise and setting off fire alarms in the hopes of obstructing the webcast as well. When Murray finished the webcast, a mob of protesters accosted him and the faculty member as they tried to exit the building, injuring the professor and giving her a concussion. Later that evening, Murray and his party were forced to flee the restaurant where they were eating because protesters had discovered their location and were following them there.[98]

Because of the injury to Middlebury professor Allison Stanger, the episode received far more attention and condemnation than might otherwise have been the case. But the fact is that such obstructions of campus speech are all too frequent.

Shortly before the Murray talk at Middlebury, the right-wing provocateur Milo Yiannopoulos was prevented from speaking at Berkeley by a violent mob that did extensive property damage, and the conservative comedian Gavin McInnes was prevented from speaking by a raucous group of protesters at New York University.[99] Shortly after the Middlebury incident, the left-wing philosopher Peter Singer was prevented from speaking at the University of Victoria in Australia by a group of disability rights protesters, and the director of the film *Boys Don't Cry* was nearly prevented by transgender activists from speaking at a screening of her film at Reed College.[100] At Claremont McKenna College, protesters declaring that they "CANNOT and WILL NOT allow fascism to have a platform" blocked the entrance to an auditorium where the writer Heather Mac Donald was to give a talk in support of modern policing.[101] At the University of California at Irvine, police had to be called to clear protesters from the Students for Justice in Palestine, who had blocked the entrances to an auditorium in which Students Supporting Israel were to show a film about the Israeli Defense Force.[102] At the University of California at Santa Barbara, a feminist studies professor led a chant of "Tear down the sign" (the sign displayed a photo of an aborted fetus) at a pro-life rally on campus before eventually grabbing and destroying the sign, explaining that as a teacher of reproductive freedom she had been "triggered" by the pro-life rally and was trying to set a good example for her students by obstructing it.[103] At Northwestern University, activists burst into an undergraduate sociology class and forced its cancellation so that a representative of the Immigration and Customs Enforcement agency was prevented from speaking to the students. The student protesters issued a statement declaring, "We do not engage in conversations with ICE in any way, shape, or form, regardless of their position," and denounced the instructor as "irresponsible" for trying to engage in a dialogue with "state actors of violence."[104] At the College of William & Mary, students identifying themselves with Black Lives Matter prevented a representative of the American Civil Liberties Union from giving a talk on the constitutional rights of protesters.[105] At Columbia University, student protesters "stormed" a class being taught by a professor of law because they objected to the role she had played in campus sexual assault investigations.[106]

The rallying cry of "stop fascists from speaking" has a long history dating from the early twentieth century in the international Left, often directed toward representatives of actual fascist political parties in European countries, but it has been a new arrival on American college campuses. Without many examples of actual fascists to obstruct, the familiar tactic has been turned against any speakers who might articulate conservative views. The gradual spread of the "no platform for fascists" approach has been apparent for quite some time. In the 1940s, British socialists shouted down and threw stones at the leaders of the British Union of Fascists so that they could not give their speeches. By the 1960s, socialists in Britain had turned the same tactics on any members of the Conservative Party who came to campus, and by the 1970s had extended the prohibition to include Jewish speakers and supporters of Israel.[107] When the feminist author Germaine Greer was scheduled to speak at Cardiff University, some students tried to have her banned for her views on transgenderism. Opponents argued both that her views "have no place in feminism and society" and that allowing her to speak on the university campus effectively "endorses her views."[108] It is hardly surprising that by the time the tactic had made its way to American campuses, the targets included a vast range of mainstream political speakers. The list of incidents of both successful and unsuccessful attempts to suppress disfavored speech and publications on American campuses in recent years is a long one.

Although it is true that such obstructionist tactics sometimes incidentally involve speech, they are not appropriately understood as the exercise of the right of free speech. It happens that the disability rights advocates at the University of Victoria used megaphones to drown out Singer's talk, but they also unplugged the projector that was broadcasting his talk (he was appearing by Skype). Before they rushed the event itself, they had lobbied the group that was sponsoring Singer's talk to drop him and then had lobbied the university's student association to revoke the group's permission to host the event on campus. It is true that the Middlebury protesters used chants to prevent Murray from talking, but they also pulled fire alarms to drive him from the building. At Reed College, the protesting students screamed obscenities at the director in an effort to shut down the talk, but they had also destroyed the posters advertising the event. In the weeks after the Yiannopoulos riot, students at Berkeley destroyed and vandalized yard signs supporting the Donald Trump presidential campaign and sandwich boards advertising the existence of the Berkeley College Republicans. At McMaster University in Canada, protesters used drums, noisemakers, and whistles to drown out a talk by University of Toronto psychologist Jordan Peterson, who had stirred controversy earlier in the year by criticizing the extension of civil rights protections to include gender identity (other speakers who were supposed to be part of a panel discussion withdrew after being threatened when the program was announced).[109] At Goldsmiths, University of London, protesters shouted at and threatened a speaker discussing blasphemy and Islam.[110] The underlying purpose of all those activities was the same, to use any means necessary to prevent the speaker from talking and the audience from hearing.

Nonetheless, obstructionist protests are sometimes confused with the exercise of free speech. A subsequent defender of the Middlebury mob argued simply that the students "have every right to shout him down," presumably because shouting was just "communication whose tone is disagreeable."[111] Students defended their actions as just an exercise of their right of "talking back."[112] When the police were called to remove the protesters at the Singer event, they declined to do so in deference to the rights to free speech of the protesters. Police at Berkeley were ordered to stand down rather than arrest the rioters at the Yiannopoulos event, in part in the name of protecting the free speech of the protesters. There are certainly pragmatic decisions to be made about how best to control an unruly mob (the Berkeley police also worried that attempting to arrest the rioters would only wind up escalating the violence), but that should not be confused with the question of whether obstructionist protesters are themselves exercising a protected right to free speech. They are not.

Students have a right to ignore speech that they find appalling and unpersuasive, or to take up the challenge to counter such speech with arguments of their own. The students at Middlebury are surely right that they are not obliged to engage with "debates on settled topics" or to "reopen discussions long ago resolved."[113] They should feel free to spend the ninety minutes scheduled for an event doing something else that they find more productive. Students routinely stay away in droves from my lectures. What they do not have the privilege to do is to insist that no one else be allowed to engage in that debate, attend that presentation, or treat those questions as unsettled or unresolved. Free speech includes the right to choose the topic to be discussed, even if no one chooses to listen. Advancements in knowledge often come through our willingness to see old debates with fresh eyes and to reconsider received wisdom. Protesters have an appropriate right to organize their own events to offer contrary arguments, to publish their own views and circulate them on campus, to take advantage of question-and-answer sessions at public lectures to challenge the views of the speaker, and to rally outside the venue of a speech to make clear to the audience that there are dissenters from the perspective being represented inside the venue. Such protest activities are consistent with tumultuous debate and the introduction into the community of a variety of competing arguments and ideas. What protesters do not have the right to do is to prevent others from speaking to a willing audience, whether the means deployed to obstruct the speech involves shouting, blowing a horn, or setting off a smoke bomb.

Constitutional law has long recognized the problem of obstructionist protests, and judges have been clear that accepting a "heckler's veto" is inconsistent with the principles of free speech. The problem was apparent to those attending the Singer event. As one reporter at the event noted, "What began as two conflicting defenses of free speech soon hindered discussion of any kind, as the Effective Altruists and protesters battled with the volume to deafening proportions."[114] Allowing obstructionist tactics to shut down speech inhibits rather than facilitates the free exchange of ideas. Rather than engaging in debate, marshaling argument, and appealing to reasoned consideration, obstructionist tactics reduce the public sphere to a set of shouting matches. In a more honest moment, defenders of such tactics admit that the protesters just "don't want to have a conversation."[115] Of course, by exercising the heckler's veto they did not merely withdraw from a conversation in which they did not want to engage; they forcibly prevented anyone else from engaging in that conversation either.

The law has come to recognize that the right to free speech can be stifled as effectively by a mob as by a censor. Not only does the government have the obligation to refrain from silencing dissenters itself; the government cannot stand idly by and allow a mob to silence the dissenter instead. The sheriff cannot shut down an unpopular speaker, but neither can the sheriff collude with the mob to shut down the speech. If speakers are acting within their rights in speaking, others have a positive duty not to interfere with the exercise of those rights. By the exact same token, if writers are within their rights to publish a newspaper or print a flyer, others have a positive duty not to destroy that property and prevent interested readers from receiving it. There is a long history in the United States of rule by mob. In the slave states prior to the Civil War, mobs routinely attacked antislavery speakers, destroyed abolitionist presses, and stole abolitionist mail.[116] The mob was no doubt expressing its own views on the slavery debate, but they were hardly within their rights to engage in such actions, and a sheriff who stood aside to allow the mob to have its way was complicit in the suppression of free speech as surely as if he were to have obstructed the abolitionists himself. We have generally counted it as progress that as a liberal democracy we have rejected such episodes of mob rule as wrong and not to be emulated. One of the great postwar First Amendment scholars, Thomas Emerson, wrote,

Up to a point heckling or other interruption of the speaker may be part of the dialogue. But conduct that obstructs or seriously impedes the utterance of another, even though

verbal in form, cannot be classified as expression. Rather
it is the equivalent of sheer noise. It has the same effect, in
preventing or disrupting communication, as acts of physical force. . . . The speaker is entitled to protection from
this form of interference as from any other physical obstruction.[117]

Judicial protection of speakers from the heckler's veto has
been crucial to the expression of dissenting opinions. It is the
most marginal, most unpopular members of society who are
most in need of protection from mob rule. In the earliest cases
of this sort that reached the US Supreme Court, it was the police who arrested speakers who the government feared would
incite a hostile crowd to violence. The threat of obstructionist
protest and possible violence, for example by segregationist
audience members, created the justification for the police to
shut down unpopular speakers like civil rights activists. It was
in part from observing the civil rights movement and the efforts of segregationists to oppose them that American judges
were led to develop more robust protections of free speech.
Once police got the message that they could not stifle a speaker
in order to preempt an angry mob, it became necessary for the
courts to further point out that neither could the police stand
passively by and allow speakers to be overwhelmed by a hostile crowd. Institutions that care about preserving the right to
free speech must take the actions necessary to ensure that the
right can in fact be exercised.

The court has emphasized that it is precisely when the
speaker is unpopular and the crowd hostile that the principle
of free speech needs to be invoked and defended. In a case
protecting the speech rights of a group of protesters critical of
President Richard Nixon, a federal circuit court summarized,

The purpose of the First Amendment is to encourage discussion, and it is intended to protect the expression of unpopular as well as popular ideas. Accordingly, hostile public
reaction does not cause the forfeiture of the constitutional
protection afforded a speaker's message so long as the
speaker does not go beyond mere persuasion and advocacy
of ideas and attempts to incite to riot.[118]

If members of the audience can shout down a speaker, destroy
a newspaper, or vandalize a sign, then the free exchange of
ideas is at an end just as surely as it would be if government
officials had arrested the speaker or confiscated the publication. The "alternative would lead to standardization of ideas
either by legislatures, courts, or dominant political or community groups."[119]

If the mission of the university is to foster vigorous debate
in order to advance our understanding of what might be true
about the world, then universities must endeavor to preserve
the conditions under which a genuine exchange of views can
take place. If members of the scholarly community are committed to intellectual inquiry and learning, then they must at
the very least be committed to refraining from silencing those
with whom they disagree. In an institution of higher education
such as Yale University, one would hope that students would at
least have the self-discipline to refrain from spitting on the
attendees at a conference on free speech that included a sit-
ting US senator and a former member of the Federal Election
Commission.[120] Mill would have hoped that in our best moments we would ourselves be willing to engage with and learn
from those with whom we disagree most strongly, but he insisted that even in our worst moments we must allow others
to engage with and learn from those with whom we disagree.

Abandoning that most basic principle of liberal tolerance condemns society to ignorance and rule by naked force. Protesters who claim the right to physically prevent speakers from speaking to a willing audience have simply invited us to settle our differences through street brawls and riots rather than through discussion and deliberation. Rather than holding up ideas for critical scrutiny, they insist that those who are more numerous or more violent are empowered to silence those who are powerless and force their obeisance. Pursuing such tactics is antithetical to the most basic commitments of a university.

## Student Groups and Outside Speakers

Universities are complicated organizations, and many of the most visible disputes about free speech on campus have involved relatively marginal features of those institutions. This is not to say that those disputes are themselves unimportant, but they should be put in perspective and we should appreciate how they relate to the larger university culture and mission.

Some of the most visible recent disputes about free speech on college campuses have focused on outside speakers. The core of the learning environment at a university can be found in the classroom, faculty offices, and the library. It is in those spaces that new research is produced and students are taught. But those do not exhaust the intellectual opportunities on a college campus. The intellectual environment on a college campus would be significantly impoverished if it were reduced to its core of formal teaching and research.

Universities routinely host myriad speakers and events on their campuses. The purposes and intended audiences for these vary greatly, as do the ways by which they are selected. Some are primarily for entertainment. Some are largely ceremonial. Some are aimed at wide audiences, and others emerge from more narrow constituencies. Together they enrich the intellectual life of the campus, though the marginal value of any given event might be relatively small.

The sheer variety of visitors can place those concerned about free speech on campus in a bit of a bind. As a practical matter, some of the visitors of greatest interest to university officials and students make the smallest contribution to the intellectual climate of the university. Administrators routinely brag to parents and prospective students about the high-profile celebrities, from politicians to newscasters to movie stars, who have recently graced the campus. In the spring, higher education news outlets are filled with announcements of planned commencement speakers. Often enticed to campus by large speaker fees and promises of honorary degrees, such figures can generally be counted on to give inoffensive and mostly content-free remarks. At best, such talks can be entertaining. The celebrity of the speaker might help draw a larger audience, which might serve to stir some institutional pride and perhaps plant a seed for future thought in the heads of some of the attendees. At worst, an apparent public relations coup can turn into a public relations embarrassment. In light of a series of sexual assault charges, the honorary degrees conferred on the comedian Bill Cosby and the commencement addresses he delivered now seem tarnished.[121] Revelations of the expense associated with bringing to campus such prominent figures as future presidential candidate Hillary Clinton, presidential offspring Donald Trump Jr., reality show notable Snooki, or movie actor Matthew McConaughey have cast a pall over what were intended to be feel-good events.[122] Protests over the selection of such speakers as President Barack Obama, Vice President Mike Pence, former Secretary of the Navy Jim Webb, former Secretary of State Condoleezza Rice, and former Secretary of State Madeleine Albright have marred what were intended to be celebratory events.[123] Seeking to avoid such missteps, some campuses have decided to cut back on speaker invitations, only to encounter complaints that universities were not doing enough to celebrate and entertain the students.[124] The controversies surrounding such speakers have become so routine that journalists now offer their readers a "definitive guide to totally unobjectionable commencement speaker picks" and previews as "disinvitation season begins."[125] In many cases, such controversies have led colleges to switch to more anodyne speakers, which might sometimes mean less intellectually engaging but generally has meant less conservative.[126]

Such controversies have put universities in a no-win situation while putting on public display the embarrassing failure of universities to sustain their core values. From the perspective of advancing and disseminating knowledge, it matters little whether former Secretary of State Condoleezza Rice or rocker Steven Van Zandt delivers the commencement address at Rutgers University.[127] It matters not at all whether rapper Big Sean performs at a spring bacchanalia at Princeton University.[128] The fact that such people have passed through campus can add a bit of luster to a glossy brochure to be mailed to prospective students, but the community of scholars who reside on campus will find their work wholly unaffected by the presence or absence of such visitors. For committees charged with the unenviable task of filling such slots on the university calendar, the aim is to seek to identify candidates who are interesting but not too interesting, well-known but not contentious, stimulating but not actually provocative. Preferably, such performers will make students feel engaged and important without actually engaging them or distracting them from other business.

Unfortunately, no matter how banal the anticipated re-marks of a commencement speaker might be, they are now likely to be regarded as more than merely ceremonial adorn-ments or occasions of uncustomary excitement. For at least some on campus, speakers will be assessed on the degree of their conformity to an ideological litmus test. The president of the United States is never to be regarded simply as a high gov-ernment official and prestigious national figure. He or she is always a policymaker and politician, whose record is to be evaluated against a preferred scorecard and, more often than not, found wanting on some dimension or another.

By itself, this is not so troubling; it could even be encourag-ing. Far better for students to be thoughtful participants in events on campus than idle spectators, and a robust culture of free speech on campus should give ample space to students to voice their discontent and disagreement with campus speak-ers. But the movement against commencement speakers is rarely limited to expressions of disagreement. Instead, they too often take the form of threats of disruption or demands for disinvitation. An announcement of a commencement speaker deemed controversial is not an occasion for debate, but is in-stead an occasion for muscle flexing.

The difficulty assuredly lies with campus administrators and campus speakers who are too gun-shy about controversy, as well as with students who are keen to insist that they not be confronted with disagreement. There is, no doubt, something to be said for the desire to avoid unnecessary confrontations over speakers for celebratory events like the annual com-mencement. But once a speaker has been selected, it does not speak well for a campus community if the response is an in-sistence that an invitation to a speaker be revoked. All too rare is the example of President Jonathan Veitch of Occidental

College. In 2016, he selected the Harvard Law School professor Randall Kennedy, a leading scholar of race and criminal justice, to serve as the commencement speaker. Kennedy had recently become embroiled in debates over the procedures by which colleges investigate charges of sexual assault by students and mete out discipline. Some faculty members and students denounced the choice as a "slap in the face," while the president defended Kennedy's selection as particularly apt in a period of activism over questions of racial justice on college campuses. Veitch insisted, however, that "calls to withdraw the invitation to Professor Kennedy reflect a disturbing trend in our national life and on college campuses—which President Obama himself has commented on—in which we are no longer willing to engage with ideas with which we disagree."[129] A local student activist group, the Coalition at Oxy for Diversity and Equity, responded that graduating seniors were being asked to "walk across the stage in the shadow of pernicious violence, cast not only by our esteemed speaker, but also by you."[130] Rather than revoking the invitation to Kennedy, Occidental instead expanded his time on campus to facilitate more conversations between Kennedy and the campus community. At Haverford College in 2014, Robert Birgeneau, the former chancellor of the University of California at Berkeley, withdrew from his planned delivery of the commencement address after students objected to his invitation given how he had dealt with protests on the Berkeley campus.[131] William Bowen, a former president of Princeton University, volunteered to take Birgeneau's place and used the occasion of his commencement address to deliver a stinging rebuke to the student activists for their intolerance and immaturity.[132] A large group of students at Bethune-Cookman University embarrassed their campus by loudly booing Education Secretary Betsy DeVos throughout her commencement address, forcing the university president to threaten ending the event early if the dissenting students could not maintain some decorum during the ceremony. Some students were removed from the event because of their disruption. Earlier in the day, DeVos had participated in a roundtable discussion with students on education issues.[133] Far better was the example of the Notre Dame students who staged a silent walkout from their commencement when Vice President Mike Pence took the podium, which allowed the students to express their dissent without disrupting the event.[134] The campus free speech watchdog group Foundation for Individual Rights in Education (FIRE) has tracked a steady rise since the onset of the twenty-first century in the number of "disinvited" campus speakers and an even faster rise in the number of activist efforts to try to force the disinvitation of speakers.[135] For many colleges across the country, the commencement address is the sole opportunity they have to attract a prominent figure to campus. The choice of speakers has also become a test for how open a campus culture actually is.

The commencement address is an unusual feature of campus life. The event itself is supposed to be ceremonial and designed to honor the graduates. The purpose of the speaker is to offer a few words of wisdom to inspire and recognize the students. Such events are not debates. They offer no ready vehicle for dialogue or contestation. The students and their parents are a captive audience in the sense that they are not there to hear the commencement address but to participate in a graduation ceremony. When speakers are particularly interesting or controversial, universities can add to the intellectual life of campus by taking advantage of their presence on campus to have supplemental events where a genuine exchange of views and substantive conversation are possible. But universities further and unnecessarily complicate the commencement by handing out honorary degrees (as Notre Dame did with Vice President Pence). As a result, the speaker chosen to deliver the commencement address is often him- or herself being honored during the event. Suddenly students are in a particular bind of becoming participants in an event to honor a speaker with whom they might disagree. A silent walkout or nearby protest of the awarding of an honorary degree to an individual deemed unworthy of being honored is a valuable expression of dissent. On the other hand, a walkout on a mere speech sends a less appealing signal that students are unwilling to even be in the presence of, let alone listen to the remarks of, someone with whom they disagree. University administrators should be more accepting of expressions of dissent, even when parents are in town, but they might also rethink the business of awarding honorary degrees. Students might likewise consider exactly what message they are sending by protesting not the content of the commencement speech but the identity of the speaker.

Such formal campus-wide events as commencement addresses are highly visible but ultimately and by design somewhat bland. More meaningful features of the intellectual life of a college campus come in less ceremonial and more targeted events. It is in those venues that speakers are invited to be provocative and develop serious arguments. The attendees at such events are expected to be interested and engaged. The events are routinely organized so as to allow an exchange of ideas, with rebuttal speakers or question-and-answer sessions. Visitors are brought to campus in order to supplement and shake up the routines of local intellectual life. Students and faculty are given the opportunity to engage with someone new and to hear a speaker bring to life arguments and perspectives that they might otherwise see only in the pages of a book or on a television screen. Many such events are likely to be largely invisible, as visitors are brought to campus to speak to individual classes or faculty workshops. Those invisible events are also closest to the scholarly mission of the university, pressing the boundaries of knowledge with a specialized audience. More public events are further removed from the realm of scholarship, but they seek to engage members of the campus community at large with issues of general concern. A thriving intellectual community makes space for a diverse array of such events.

Many of the more recent controversies over speakers on campus have involved these sorts of more focused groups, often student groups. The university faculty has an interest in bringing to campus scholars who are working on the frontiers of knowledge, and who, it is hoped, can convey some of that knowledge to a broader audience. Unsurprisingly, students are somewhat less interested in the cutting edge of academic research. This does not necessarily mean that they are uninterested in ideas or in learning, but their appetite is more likely to be whetted by the kinds of topics, issues, and arguments that occupy the public sphere than by those that occupy the pages of academic journals. Of course, classroom conversations often take the same form. The excitement of undergraduate teaching generally comes from introducing students to ideas that are novel to them but familiar to experts in the field. College offers students an opportunity to explore a range of ideas, to trace the course of intellectual debates, and to learn how to critically examine the claims that they encounter and to keep an open mind when they come across the unexpected.

The modern college campus has long sought to provide a venue for public debate as well as scholarly disputes. The US Supreme Court has noted the constitutional significance of this decision for state universities, but the core point has broader application for any university that cares about free speech. When thinking about free speech on government property, the court has often asked what kind of "forum" the government property is as a practical matter. Some government property, like a public park, is a traditional public forum where free speech is relatively unrestricted. Some property, like a Social Security administrative office, is not a public forum at all, and the government is free to restrict access to it. Some property that might not traditionally be regarded as a public forum could nonetheless become a designated public forum. As a consequence such property is made available to the public for assembly and debate, and the government must respect robust protections for free speech. In particular, the government is obliged to be "content neutral" in how it regulates speech in such public spaces. The university can help coordinate how campus space and resources are used, and can prevent student activities from interfering with the operation of the university, but a college cannot bar student speech simply because university officials do not approve of it, nor can they impose restrictions on that speech that render it ineffective and pointless.

State college campuses are generally recognized as designated public fora. A college might restrict the use of its buildings to students, for example, but it cannot favor some instances of student speech over others or place onerous restrictions on how students might make use of the space. Universities routinely require student groups to be officially recognized in order to reserve campus space, distribute publications and flyers on campus, or access funds for activities, but they are required to recognize groups in an evenhanded fashion. Once recognized, all student groups must be treated the same and allowed to equally enjoy the benefits associated with being a recognized student group. When the president of Central Connecticut State College refused to allow students to create a local chapter of the Students for a Democratic Society, a prominent New Left activist group at the center of many disruptive protests in the 1960s, the US Supreme Court emphasized the importance of giving a wide scope to student-led debate on campus. College officials could not burden or ban a student group because it espoused "repugnant" views or preached "doing away with any or all campus regulations." A college could discipline students if and when they violate "reasonable campus rules, interrupt classes, or substantially interfere with the opportunity of other students to obtain an education," but it could not prevent them from engaging in advocacy.[136] Similarly, when the University of Virginia denied access to a generally available student activities fund to a student group that wanted to publish a campus magazine offering a "Christian perspective" on campus life, the court emphasized that the university could not play favorites in providing resources to student groups. Having made funds available to student groups to create campus publications, the university may not engage in "viewpoint discrimination" and place unequal burdens on the speech of some students because of the "specific motivating ideology or the opinion or perspective of the speaker."[137] When Oregon State University confiscated the distribution bins of the conservative student paper that had been placed next to the bins of the official school paper and other independent papers, a federal circuit court curtly observed, "We have little trouble finding constitutional violations" in the university's actions.[138] When Texas A&M University refused to recognize Gay Student Services as a student group, and the University of Southern Mississippi refused to recognize a chapter of the Mississippi Civil Liberties Union, a federal circuit court emphasized that once a university has opened its campus to a wide range of student groups, it cannot prohibit groups offering a competing message, even when that message is unpopular, offensive in the eyes of university administrators or alumni, or at odds with the government's own laws then on the books.[139] Even private universities have opened themselves up to litigation by adopting a similar commitment to equal freedom of inquiry and advocacy but then failing to live up to it, as Fordham University has done in denying recognition to a local chapter of Students for Justice in Palestine because the club would lead to "polarization" on campus.[140]

The records of legal cases amply demonstrate that administrators at public colleges have often tried to stifle student groups of which they disapprove. Officials at private colleges have been no less assiduous in their efforts to shut down disfavored speakers and students, but they do not face the same constitutional limitations on their actions and so do not as often come under judicial scrutiny. These cases illustrate why the evenhanded treatment of student activities is a necessary implication of free speech principles. In the years after the civil rights movement, judges found it hard to ignore the extent to which students had political opinions of their own and sought to express them. Once the court recognized that students had rights, the arbitrary denigration of those rights by school officials was unsustainable.

Just as important, judges came to appreciate how the college campus had become a significant site for vigorous debate over the social issues of the day. Classroom discussions under faculty supervision are not the only vehicle for learning. The "marketplace of ideas" includes student-led activities where new ideas could be explored, tested, discarded, and embraced.

When the University of Mississippi tried to close down a student-run literary magazine in the early 1970s because its "tasteless and inappropriate" language was offensive to the community and threatened to embarrass the school in the eyes of the public and the legislature, a federal circuit court reminded school officials that they could no more censor a student literary journal for publishing offensive poetry or short stories than they could censor a law review for publishing controversial articles on abortion or desegregation. Censorious campus officials were in danger of sacrificing "the historical role of the University in expressing opinions which may well not make favor with the majority of society and in serving in the vanguard in the fight for freedom and expression and opinion."[141] To the officials at the Virginia Commonwealth University who wanted to ban the Gay Alliance of Students for promoting "abhorrent, even sickening" ideas and behavior, a circuit court pointed out that "student associations devoted to advocacy of political, social, legal and other objectives are part of higher education and useful in preparation for later life." While individual university officials, campus chaplains, instructors, and students could forcefully advocate for their own preferred values, those arguments must compete in the marketplace of ideas, and students were free to choose whether or not to accept them. University administrators dedicated to liberal education and democratic ideals must tolerate the presence of "associations devoted to peaceful advocacy of decriminalization or social acceptance of sadism, euthanasia, masochism, murder, genocide, segregation, master-race theories, gambling, voodoo, and the abolishment of higher education" even if those ideas were as offensive to them as advocacy of tolerance of homosexuality.[142] When the legislature of the state of Alabama prohibited any student group from having access to public funds or facilities if it "fosters or promotes a lifestyle or actions prohibited by the sodomy and sexual misconduct laws," a federal court observed that the statute unconstitutionally impaired the activities of the Gay Lesbian Bisexual Alliance at the University of South Alabama in the same ways that hate speech laws interfered with student advocacy.[143]

Student-led groups and their associated activities have become vital components of the educational mission of the modern university. They are not asked to meet the disciplinary standards expected of members of the faculty and courses incorporated into the curriculum, but they supplement those more scholarly features of the university and serve as a bridge between the university community and the larger social and political world. It is conceivable that a university could decide to forgo such groups entirely and restrict campus activities to faculty-led events, but something important would be lost in the process. The intellectual life of the campus would be significantly narrowed, student interests would be neglected, and important debates within the larger public sphere would be inadequately vetted on campus.

At the same time, we should recognize what student groups contribute to a campus and what they do not. The faculty hired to teach and research at a university are evaluated by their peers for the quality of their understanding of their disciplinary subject. We think the pursuit of truth can be advanced through the rigorous evaluation of scholarly work and would-be scholars, and the certification of those that can pass through those fires and demonstrate their worth. We do not expect the same from student groups and campus speakers. We would hope that a student gets better, and not just different, information from taking a course in the sociology department than from attending a speaker series sponsored by the College Republicans. That does not mean that the latter is not worthwhile, but it should be taken for what it is. If the university were to close down the student group's speaker series, asserting that students should not get mixed messages by having their course content challenged by outside speakers, then we would rightfully worry about whether the university has the courage of its convictions.

Having embraced the vision of the college campus as an open forum of debate, university officials cannot be selective in what arguments and perspectives they are willing to let in. It would be extraordinarily shortsighted to imagine that university officials would always align themselves with the forces of progress if given free rein to skew that debate. Armed with the power to censor, university administrators have proven themselves very willing to suppress viewpoints and forms of expression that they find immoral, embarrassing, offensive, indecent, misguided, or simply unpopular and inconvenient. Of course, university officials are rarely willing to say explicitly that they want to exclude some ideas from campus. Instead they have relied on vague standards that give them ample discretion to single out particular student groups as inconsistent with campus values, while continuing to maintain that the campus is open to free inquiry. When it has been too embarrassing for university administrators themselves to suppress disfavored groups, they have delegated the task to others, such as members of the student government. But whether the decision of which groups to recognize or how to distribute student activity funds is made by an assistant dean, the president of the student government, or a vote of the student body, the effect of stifling dissenting views and closing off debate is the same. When the Wichita State University student president declared that the members of the student government must "do what they see as best for the institution," including refusing to recognize a chapter of the Young Americans for Liberty, if the majority "feel that an organization can be detrimental to Wichita State University," he simply echoed the sentiments of the president of Virginia Commonwealth University when he refused to recognize the Gay Alliance of Students a generation earlier.[144] Both, no doubt, hoped to spare their university controversy, but they did so by sacrificing the ideal of free inquiry and debate on which the modern university is founded (as well as violating the requirements of the US Constitution).

The effort to squash student-led groups that introduce controversial ideas to campus is hardly a thing of the past. In the 1960s and 1970s, university administrators were frequently inclined to try to drive out advocates of black civil rights, women's liberation, gay rights, and socialism. More recently, advocates of conservative causes from evangelical Christians to economic libertarians have been more likely to provoke the ire of university officials. It is often these groups that challenge campus orthodoxy and encourage campus debate over political and social causes, and their opponents have responded by trying to deny them official recognition, access to campus facilities, and opportunities to make use of common funds. At the extreme, opponents of such groups have tried not only to disband and silence them but even to expel their members from the university. In doing so, they admit that they would prefer not to have their own beliefs challenged and tested, and would prefer that other members of the campus community not be exposed to dissenting perspectives. They prefer "dead dogma" to "living truth."

There are, however, important questions to be asked about how scarce resources are actually expended. While all students should be equally free to take advantage of campus resources to publicize and investigate ideas and issues of interest to them, this does not mean that students do not have a responsibility of their own to make a productive contribution to the search for knowledge. If the value of free speech for the university community is its ability to help us make progress toward better understanding the world and sharing that understanding with others, then we make the best use of free speech when we contribute toward those goals. As a tolerant liberal and democratic society, we make space for speech simply as self-expression, or self-indulgence, and the First Amendment has been interpreted to secure that space. The university community is not a democracy, however. It is a community forged for a particular purpose, to facilitate learning, and free speech is valuable to that community and for that purpose because of its connection to the search for truth. If we abandon that search, then free speech becomes mostly pointless within the specific context of a university.

There is a temptation to press up against the boundaries of free speech just for the sake of pushing boundaries. There are sometimes benefits to doing so, but often such activities just stir controversy with little promise of compensating gain. No doubt stirring controversy can sometimes be fun, and it can certainly attract an audience, perhaps disproportionately from the college-age demographic. Many have taken advantage of that fact over time, and some have provided more insight while doing so than others. Comedians like Lenny Bruce, George Carlin, and Andrew Dice Clay, "shock jocks" like Howard Stern, performance artists like Karen Finley, professional provocateurs like Milo Yiannopoulos and Ann Coulter, pornographers like Larry Flynt, satirists like the artists and writers for *Mad* magazine and *Charlie Hebdo* have entertained and excited their fans by being self-consciously offensive. By defying conventions of polite society and holding sacred cows up for ridicule, they make a point and tear down barriers, but such efforts often come at a cost. Civil libertarians often find themselves defending such provocative figures in order to hold the line on a zone of permissible free speech and to disempower the censor, but it would be a mistake to celebrate them as heroes. Free speech is not defended for the benefit of provocateurs; they are parasitic on free speech. When free speech principles are challenged, they must be defended, but it would be a mistake to reduce free speech to a defense of provocateurs. Though it might be tempting to provoke free speech battles by inviting shocking figures to campus, there is in general little reason for doing so. Those are cheap thrills. If free speech battles are to be had, they are better fought for prizes worth taking. The payoff for insisting that a university respect the equal right of all students to organize, advocate, and explore ideas should be something more substantively valuable than a campus visit by Milo Yiannopoulos.

Similarly, student groups should consider the depth of intellectual content that can be gained by a particular event or speaker. In organizing events, students generally are not putting together a philosophy seminar. They are, as the circuit court in the Virginia Commonwealth University case noted, concerned with advocacy on the issues that are current in public life, and with preparing for life outside the university. Moreover, they are competing for the attention of their fellow students, who have on offer not only study time in the library but also party time in the fraternity. As such, they cannot be expected to shy away from public figures and popular issues. The Young Americans for Liberty should not be expected to invite in the same speakers as the Department of Political Science. But within that context, groups should consider what the available speakers have to offer. Without a doubt, the white nationalist Richard Spencer and former Ku Klux Klan Grand Wizard David Duke are a part of the world, and students might gain some insights from being exposed to their arguments, but they are, to be generous, marginal figures in American politics and not particularly insightful critics of civil rights liberalism. By giving such figures a platform, students give them a prominence that they have not earned. By focusing limited resources and attention on minor celebrities, students are missing an opportunity to grapple with more serious thinkers and more challenging ideas.

Even Richard Spencer and Ann Coulter have an absolute right to be heard in American society. They do not necessarily need or deserve a space on a college campus to advance their arguments. Given a range of options, they should not be the first choice for those seeking to hear from thoughtful advocates of the contesting positions on the issues of the day. John Stuart Mill counseled that we should seek out the strongest arguments of our opponents, as well as of our friends, for they will be most helpful in guiding us to the opinions that we should adopt as our own, and in challenging us to develop the best supports for those opinions. When we are making decisions about whom to invite to campus to speak, the goal should be neither to stack the deck with our closest allies nor to sprinkle in the most extreme provocateurs. The goal should be to make available to the campus community thoughtful representatives of serious ideas. Certainly those ideas that are well within the mainstream of contemporary American life should be amply represented, but a university community benefits as well from considering ideas that are currently on the margins but have the potential to be of significant consequence in the future. Universities are centrally concerned with considering alternatives to the status quo. Assessing the merits of those alternatives, however, requires grappling with them not as caricatures but in their strongest form.

It would be an unfortunate situation, but a remediable one, if controversies over campus speakers were limited to provocateurs and fringe celebrities. Such is not the case. Instead faculty and student activists have taken to objecting to even mainstream, substantive speakers who do not fit within the narrow confines of their preferred orthodoxy. An open letter by a group of Pomona College students defended the obstructionist protest of conservative writer Heather Mac Donald at nearby Claremont McKenna College. Mac Donald's views are certainly controversial, but she is an influential writer at a mainstream conservative think tank who develops serious arguments. Her presence at a congressional hearing, on a national newspaper's editorial page, on a PBS talk show, or in a public library speaker series would hardly raise an eyebrow, and yet she is regarded as beyond the pale on some college campuses. The Pomona students explained their objections to Mac Donald's presence on campus by arguing that free speech "has recently become a tool appropriated by hegemonic institutions." It is one thing for "students from marginalized backgrounds" to use it "to voice their qualms and criticize aspects of the institution," but it is quite another for it to be used by "those who seek to perpetuate systems of domination." Mac Donald is a "white supremacist fascist supporter of the police state," and allowing her to disseminate her "toxic and deadly illogic" is tantamount to "condoning violence against Black people." Engaging with her in the name of free inquiry, indeed the "the idea that the truth is an entity for which we must search," is "an attempt to silence oppressed peoples."[145] In response to a speech delivered on campus by Laura Kipnis, a group of Wellesley College faculty issued a statement calling for the end of such controversial speakers. That view was quickly endorsed by the student newspaper. Kipnis is a well-known "pro-sex feminist" and professor of media studies at Northwestern University, who produced a trade book with a major publishing house on debates over campus policies relating to sexual conduct, including a controversial case in which Kipnis became entangled on her own campus. This was the topic of her talk at Wellesley. In response, the faculty statement decried such speakers who "impose on the liberty of students, staff, and faculty at Wellesley." Members of the Wellesley community experienced "distress as a result of a speaker's words" and felt compelled to "invest time and energy in rebutting the speakers' arguments." The members of the faculty Commission for Ethnicity, Race, and Equity called for all future potential speaker invitations to be vetted by them first.[146] In the wake of public reaction to the faculty letter, the Wellesley student newspaper editorialized that only "viable discourse" should be allowed on campus, and free speech existed only "to protect the disenfranchised and . . . the suppressed, not to protect a free-for-all where anything is acceptable." The students admitted that sometimes "mistakes will happen and controversial statements will be said," but insisted that if community members making such mistakes "refuse to adapt their beliefs, then hostility may be warranted," and they should be held "accountable." Outsiders like "paid professional lecturers and politicians" did not even deserve the opportunity to mend their ways or to be heard; they deserved only "beration."[147]

A campus that seeks to plug its ears against the possibility of hearing "controversial statements" has abandoned the scholarly enterprise. It is seeking to withdraw from the world not in order to create a safe space for free inquiry but in order to create an alternative reality free from disagreements over important aspects of the human condition. Such reactions to controversial speakers epitomize the "free speech for me, but not for thee" attitude held by political and religious authorities throughout much of human history, an attitude that the liberal tradition sought to displace. John Milton, John Locke, and John Stuart Mill well understood that the only effective way to secure free speech for "the suppressed" was to insist that free speech should be available to everyone. Would the Wellesley faculty Commission for Ethnicity, Race, and Equity be equally comfortable if all potential speakers had to be vetted by the local conservative professor before being invited to campus? Should a conservative professor likewise be empowered to reject all those potential speakers who he or she thought were likely to advance shopworn, politically dangerous, or ill-conceived ideas? Undoubtedly, the symmetrical application of such restrictive speech policies would soon become grating for those who currently advocate for them. As has always been the case, it is only those who plan to monopolize the power to censor who find censorship to be an attractive idea. Those who are genuinely powerless or marginal in a given community have always preferred that the freedom of critical inquiry be uncompromised. We have managed to make progress, intellectually and politically, when the powerful have been made to respect the freedom of the powerless and to let their voices be heard as well.

One of the odd features of the Wellesley faculty statement in response to the Kipnis speech is how it blurred the difference between outside speakers and members of the faculty. The statement raises the question of who "is actually qualified for the platform granted by an invitation to Wellesley." As I have noted, it is important to think through the value added to campus discussion of any potential speaker before an invitation is extended (once the invitation has been extended, free speech principles indicate that it should be honored except in the most extraordinary circumstances). But the Wellesley statement frames that issue as one of qualifications and is even more particularly concerned with "whether the presenter has standing in his/her/their discipline." The expressed concern is that the college should avoid inviting speakers who peddle in "pseudoscience," though the implication seems to really be that disfavored substantive arguments should be excluded.[148]

Are there qualifications to be an outside speaker on a college campus? It seems implausible, beyond the general requirement of being substantively interesting and being able to contribute to the community's understanding of public events. The Wellesley statement was reacting specifically to the visit by Laura Kipnis, though it refrained from referencing her directly. Kipnis is a tenured professor in the School of Communications at Northwestern University who has built her career around the study of the cultural politics of sex. If the Wellesley statement meant to deny that Professor Kipnis had adequate standing to critique the politics of sex on college campuses, then the attack seems misdirected. But laying aside the specific case of Kipnis, do we or should we require that visiting speakers on campus have appropriate "standing" within their discipline? If so, the frequent college appearances by Noam Chomsky, a distinguished linguist but a popular speaker on American foreign policy, or Robert Reich, a former labor secretary and frequent public commentator on economics but uncredentialed in the dismal science, would seem to be suspect. Or consider the case of Donald Trump's international trade adviser, University of California at Irvine economics professor Peter Navarro. He has carved out a successful public career as a polemicist on trade issues, but is unlikely to be sought out for a faculty appointment as a trade economist. It would be foolish, however, to conclude that there is nothing to be gained from hearing a public lecture by a man who has the ear of the president, even if the audience will have to wade through a great deal of error in the process. If students wished to hear from Dr. Mehmet Oz—a distinguished heart surgeon who has won fame and fortune as a television celebrity dispensing dubious medical advice that might generously be labeled pseudoscience—it seems unlikely that the Wellesley faculty would object. Michael Albert is an advocate of a radical "participatory economy" and a favored thinker associated with the Occupy Wall Street movement, but would be unlikely to get much of a hearing from the faculty of a college economics department. Thomas Sowell is a trained economist and one of the most prominent black conservative intellectuals of the 1980s, but he made his living in think tanks and op-ed pages rather than academic departments. Should students be prohibited from inviting such speakers to campus because some on campus might feel the need to rebut their arguments, or should only Sowell be prohibited because the particular "systems of domination" that he has dedicated his career to dismantling are not the ones the Pomona students had in mind?

Universities have used a variety of procedures to regulate the speakers that are brought to campus. Preferably, those procedures are designed to accomplish the admirable purpose of making effective and efficient use of university resources and providing all students with fair and equitable access to those resources. Unfortunately, sometimes those procedures are used to obstruct rather than facilitate the exchange of ideas. Some colleges require that student groups secure faculty advisers. Sometimes they require that members of the faculty agree before any invitations are extended to outside speakers. Such requirements can be sensible and useful, but they become problematic if they serve as a backdoor means of filtering out some potential student groups and their visitors. Similarly, bureaucratic red tape can be used to selectively silence groups that don't meet with the favor of campus administrators. Admittedly, students can sometimes be neglectful in satisfying bureaucratic procedures. But if administrators selectively seize on such oversights as a pretext for squashing activities that they find potentially controversial or undesirable, then the university will have turned away from its primary mission. The president of Texas Southern University rushed to the law school to shut down an event sponsored by the conservative Federalist Society—an event that had been approved by the law school administration but was being obstructed by student protesters—and American University's administrators canceled at the last minute a libertarian student group's panel of speakers: such incidents raise doubts about whether campus administrators are always acting faithfully to promote a diverse range of free speech on campus.[149] Regrettably, the disruptive activities of protesters have led to quite exorbitant security costs for some campus speakers.[150] Universities committed to free speech have an obligation to provide adequate security to ensure that such speech can take place. Imposing the security costs on the speaker or on those issuing the invitation has the effect of empowering protesters to effectively block such speakers from campus, but colleges can themselves become overwhelmed if those costs become too high. Universities might find themselves in the unenviable position of reducing access to campus in order to manage such costs. The resulting reduction of speech on campus must be laid at the feet of those who by their disruptive actions make such security necessary. The university's responsibility will be to ration available resources in a neutral and equitable manner.

Some outside speakers also come to campus uninvited. That is to a certain degree unavoidable because college campuses open themselves to the general public. Outsiders take advantage of that openness. Street preachers and small activist groups have long traveled to college campuses to get their message out to curious onlookers. Over time, colleges have acted to restrict the access of outsiders so that they are not unduly disruptive to the normal operations of the university. Recently, outside groups have more systematically targeted American university campuses, with unsettling results. After white supremacists marched through the campus of the University of Virginia (and a woman was killed during riots the next day in the town of Charlottesville) in the summer of 2017, administrators were forced to reevaluate their rules regarding the access of outsiders to university grounds and reasonably sought to take steps to keep mass protesters away from the living quarters of students.[151] Other campuses have discovered the downside of offering their campus facilities for public rental as white supremacists have begun to take advantage of such accommodations to insert themselves into campus uninvited.[152] Excluding such speakers would, in some cases, require colleges to significantly alter their relationship to the general public and pull in their welcome mat to outsiders in general. Universities have generally benefited from maintaining a relatively open attitude toward outsiders who seek to engage with members of the campus community, even though such outsiders can sometimes be a nuisance and a distraction. That calculus could change, however, if the openness of college campuses is systematically exploited by outsiders who care little about the mission of the university or the degree to which its operations are disrupted.[153]

## Faculty and Academic Freedom

Outside speakers add to the vibrancy of intellectual life on a college campus, but at the scholarly center of a university is its own faculty. The notion of academic freedom was developed over the course of the twentieth century to protect this vital core of the modern university. Academic freedom is a specialized application of general free speech principles, and incorporates an important set of both rights and duties that should be respected by the campus community. Those rights and duties are designed to foster the productive exchange of ideas, the careful scrutinizing of claims, and the development of the expertise needed both to teach students and to convey what has been learned to the broader world.

Universities strive to recruit and hire faculty who are experts in their chosen fields of study and who are capable of making meaningful contributions to the advancement of knowledge in that field and competently teaching students the store of knowledge that field encompasses. The principles of academic freedom are designed to guarantee the ability of members of the faculty to engage in those tasks. The 1940 Statement of Principles on Academic Freedom and Tenure adopted by the American Association of University Professors is a canonical expression of the concept. The statement declared that professors should have "full freedom in research and in the publication of results" and "freedom in the classroom in discussing their subject," and should be "free from institutional censorship or discipline" when acting as citizens in the public sphere. Alongside the assertion of those freedoms was the recognition that members of a university faculty had a professional obligation "not to introduce into their teaching controversial matter which has no relation to their subject," and to strive when acting in the public sphere to be accurate, to "exercise appropriate restraint," to respect others, and to be clear that they do not speak for the institution.[154]

In short, the concept of academic freedom asserts that professors should be free to pursue the production and communication of their expert knowledge in accord with professional standards as set forth and evaluated by their professional peers. Faculty members are not to be punished by university administrators or trustees for the research questions that they choose to pursue or the conclusions that they reach. They are not to be directed on what to teach or how to teach it. They are not to be disciplined for speaking out about internal matters of university policy and governance or external matters of public concern.

The underlying rationale for these principles is that they are necessary to preserve the conditions for free inquiry and the pursuit of truth within the university setting. They emerged out of struggle by education reformers at the turn of the twentieth century to commit universities to the unbridled search for knowledge. Edward A. Ross was one of the founding figures of the modern discipline of sociology and a vocal advocate of immigration restrictions (a policy thought damaging to the railroad empire that produced the wealth that helped endow Stanford University). In 1900, Jane Stanford wrote to the president of the university, "I am weary of Professor Ross," and directed that his employment be terminated at the end of the semester. Ross was sent packing. In 1915, the trustees of the Wharton Business School at the University of Pennsylvania overrode the recommendation of the faculty and fired Scott Nearing, whose writing and teaching on socialism were "entirely inconsistent with Mr. Wharton's well-known views and in defiance of the conservative opinions of men of affairs." In 1929, the curators of the University of Missouri terminated Howard DeGraff for conducting a study of the sexual attitudes of college undergraduates, declaring that they had a responsibility to preserve the university as "a place to which parents may send their children with full confidence that the surrounding moral atmosphere will be sane and wholesome."[155] Such cases became notorious, and university presidents and faculty successfully pushed trustees to the sidelines in order to make the college campus a safe space for vigorous debate and scientific advancement. The quality and value of scholarly work was to be judged by other scholars with expertise in the field, not by the donors and alumni. The office of professor was to be held in public trust in order to enhance human knowledge, and not at the discretionary will of university paymasters. The principles and protective institutions of academic freedom are built on the faith that society as a whole will benefit from free inquiry and experimentation, even when particular instances of those pursuits create discomfort or seem misguided.

Within that framework of academic freedom, faculty members have a responsibility to maintain and enforce professional discipline. The faculty is indeed expected to weed out pseudo-science from within its ranks. The teaching and writing of professors like Ross, Nearing, and DeGraff were controversial. In hindsight, they might even appear to have been mistaken. But within the context of their time, they were not unprofessional. Those men were deploying the tools of their disciplines to push the boundaries of what was known within their respective fields of study, and the fruits of their efforts were of public interest and relevant not only to nearby scholars but also to policymakers and activists. If Nearing's arguments about socialism were to be found wanting, it should be because they had been scrutinized and tested by the economics profession, not because they ran afoul of the personal views and financial interest of mining magnate Joseph Wharton.

Academic freedom secures for faculty members a carefully constrained freedom of speech. They have earned the "platform" of the post of professor at a university not by gaining some notoriety in the public sphere but by demonstrating the qualifications of expertise and by making careful, measured contributions to their field of study. In order to keep it, they have a professional responsibility not to abuse it. If their writings and arguments do not meet professional standards of quality, the scholarly world has an obligation to refrain from providing venues for communicating that work. Scholarly journals and presses should refuse to publish their writings. Universities and professional conferences should decline to invite them to give presentations to the scholarly community. They have a responsibility not to use their time in the classroom to proselytize to students on subjects irrelevant to the course, and not to mislead their students on the accepted knowledge of the field. The university is under no obligation to shelter in its geography department someone who believes the earth is flat, or provide space in its astronomy department for someone who believes the sun revolves around the earth. A geologist who insisted on teaching students that the earth is less than ten thousand years old—as a substantial percentage of the American population believes but that the geology profession uniformly rejects—would be engaged in professional misconduct. A chemist who dedicates substantial class time to opining on presidential elections is in breach of her professional responsibilities. Perhaps a student group would have reason to invite an advocate of Young Earth theory to give a presentation on campus in order to hear such views elaborated and defended, but the faculty of the university would have little reason to sponsor such an event. Perhaps the students would be entertained by a lecture by a self-proclaimed expert on Bigfoot, but the biology department would be unlikely to foot the bill. The local student chapter of the Socialist Alternative might find it enlightening to hear from an advocate for workers' collectives, but the economics department is likely to think its time and resources are better spent elsewhere. The College Republicans might be excited to hear from Ann Coulter; the faculty members of the political science department would not be. At the scholarly core of the university, the faculty is expected to exercise discretion over what speech to facilitate and to engage in so as to use limited resources as efficiently as possible in order to make progress in the scholarly enterprise.

At the same time, members of the faculty have a right to be evaluated based on the performance of their professional duties and not on their privately held opinions. University officials and students should expect the professor of computer science both to refrain from teaching Christian theology in the introductory programming class and to offer competent instruction in the subject at hand. Universities have an obligation to correct professors who stray from that professional task. If a professor of electrical engineering spends his private time dallying in Holocaust denial, however, the university has an obligation only to ensure that such activity does not affect how he conducts his teaching or scholarly research.[156] Such a professor no doubt hampers rather than helps our understanding of the Holocaust, and his arguments should be vigorously exposed as erroneous, but universities should refuse to get into the business of policing the private political and social views of their faculty. If there is evidence that a professor, for whatever reason, treats students unfairly or introduces irrelevant or flagrantly wrong material into the classroom, then action should be taken to uphold appropriate professional standards. But if, regardless of the quality of their scholarship and teaching, members of the faculty can be driven from campus because they write a blog that some find vile and offensive, or belong to an unpopular religious or political group, then administrators will be empowered to hound the unorthodox and faculty will be discouraged from exploring heretical ideas. Authorizing administrators to sanction and suppress whenever a member of the faculty "goes too far" will inevitably invest them with a license to root out those who are merely out of step. Empowering university deans and presidents to purge campuses of professors who they happen to think "poison the well in the market-place of ideas" leaves the intellectual freedom on campus vulnerable to the personal predilections and wisdom of whoever happens to be in charge at the moment.[157] Tolerating a diversity of opinions will necessarily mean tolerating some deeply mistaken opinions, but a culture of conformity is antithetical to the vigorous pursuit of the truth.

Happily, the academic freedom of faculty members is better secured now than it was even in the middle of the twentieth century. Unfortunately, threats to academic freedom have not gone away and can still be found from sources both within and outside the university. Notably, one of the key structural supports for the freedom of faculty to execute their professional responsibilities in their teaching and research is the tenure system. The 1940 AAUP Statement of Principles conjoined a commitment to academic freedom to tenure. The requirement that faculty members be "terminated only for adequate cause" was designed to make it harder for college presidents to do as Stanford's did with Edward Ross in 1900: remove them from campus when their arguments become inconvenient to the economic or cultural commitments of influential donors. Tenured faculty members could still be removed for neglect or abuse of their position, but they could not be let go simply because they had become disagreeable or offensive.

In the early twenty-first century, tenure-line faculty make up an ever-shrinking proportion of the instructional staff at American universities. Contingent or adjunct instructors make an important contribution to college campuses. They can provide flexibility in addressing sudden fluctuations in student demand for curricular subjects, and they can bring the practical know-how of working professionals into college classrooms. But university administrators have also relied on contingent faculty to cut costs, undermine faculty governance, and reorganize the curriculum. This growing army of contingent faculty enjoy none of the procedural protections of academic freedom that the tenure system provides, and often have little access to the time and resources they would need to conduct research and make advancements in knowledge. It is a simple matter for university administrators to decline, without explanation, to renew the semester-by-semester contract of an adjunct instructor, even when the motivation for the dismissal is that the instructor is holding students to a higher academic standard than a dean would prefer, or assigning course readings that an assistant dean finds provocative, or has published a scholarly paper that an administrator deems to be controversial or counter to the economic interests of a prospective donor. Meanwhile, on many campuses, administrators have taken over significant swaths of the undergraduate curriculum and staffed those classes with contingent faculty outside the purview of disciplinary departments. The increasing reliance on contingent faculty on college campuses shrinks the protected sphere of academic freedom and undermines the willingness and ability of professors to produce and disseminate knowledge in accord with professional disciplinary standards.

While tenure helps protect faculty from outside pressure to conform and shade their teaching and research to fit the political needs of the university, it is not by itself sufficient to secure academic freedom. On the one hand, some members of the faculty invite attacks on the autonomy of the academic sphere by abusing their position and ignoring the type of responsibilities that the AAUP statement highlighted, such as the need to refrain from using the classroom to proselytize on unrelated subjects, or to exercise restraint and respect when speaking out as citizens with extramural speech. Academic freedom is not a blanket get-out-of-jail-free card that excuses bad behavior by professors. On the other hand, there are many both inside and outside the university who evidence little respect for the basic principles of academic freedom and instead try to influence research and teaching or punish faculty for stepping outside the bounds of approved opinions. The basic university mission of the pursuit of truth is compromised when faculty members are told that they must shy away from saying what they think is correct.

Unfortunately, students often display little understanding of these basic principles. A Harvard op-ed writer decried the "liberal obsession with 'academic freedom'" and called on universities to censor and fire faculty members, such as the conservative Harvard political science professor Harvey Mansfield, who insisted on publishing "offensive" views that were contrary to the student's sense of "social justice."[158] At Oberlin

College, hundreds of students signed on to a list of "demands" that included dropping academic requirements, altering course content, immediately promoting to tenure named faculty members, and firing other tenured faculty members.[159] At Pomona College, sociology students denounced the "undemocratic, covert hiring processes" that the department used to fill faculty positions; demanded that the visiting professorship of Alice Goffman be rescinded because her ethnographic work on young men in the Philadelphia inner city represented a white woman "theoriz[ing] about and profit[ing] from Black lives"; and insisted that undergraduate students be at the "forefront of all current and future hiring decisions" in order to guarantee that the department would hire only *"authentic mentors."*[160] At Yale University, students made headlines when a video appeared of them screaming at Professor Nicholas Christakis for comments his wife had made encouraging students to resolve their own disagreements over offensive Halloween costumes. As Christakis tried to talk to the students about the issue, students yelled, "He doesn't deserve to be listened to!"; "Who the fuck hired you? You should step down!"; and "You are disgusting!" The students subsequently rallied for the dismissal of the Christakis couple.[161]

Most regrettable are those instances when those who have the experience to know better try to intervene in what professors teach and research, and punish them for their opinions. It is perhaps reassuring that the pressure for such interventions often comes from those outside the campus community, but too often university officials and faculty aid and abet those efforts to subvert the freedom of the faculty to pursue their professional responsibilities. The historian Alice Dreger resigned from her position at Northwestern University after the dean of the medical school censored a bioethics journal she edited for fear that an article about sex and the disabled might be embarrassing to the institution. When other faculty members objected, the dean relented on the particular article but subsequently created an oversight board that included a member of the public-relations staff to approve future issues of the journal.[162] State legislators have threatened to withhold state funds from colleges that continued to teach controversial courses on race or social justice.[163] The University of North Carolina has found itself in an ongoing brawl with the Republican political leadership in the state. The politically appointed board of governors resolved to close several research centers on campus that were seen as hostile to the political and policy interests of the legislative majority, including most notably an antipoverty center in the law school, a decision the dean denounced as an attack on all those "who believe that free speech and open inquiry are indispensable tools in addressing society's greatest problems." Two years later, the board adopted a prohibition on centers in the law school, notably its civil rights center, from filing legal claims or motions. Board members argued that such litigation "does not provide the best means or a necessary means for educating law students," while faculty members argued that such hands-on litigation experience and legal advocacy work are an essential part of the law school's mission and integral to effective legal training.[164] In Virginia, the state attorney general joined in efforts to harass the atmospheric scientist Michael Mann for his research on climate change, leading to extended litigation that eventually resulted in the state high court rejecting the attorney general's investigation.[165]

In the middle of the twentieth century, university faculty members were frequently threatened with censure and dismissal for what is sometimes characterized as their "extramural" speech. What they said in the public sphere, whether on campus, at political rallies, or in newspaper op-eds, became the basis for sanctioning them when they became too controversial in the eyes of the university administration, donors, alumni, or politicians. Such public speech often does not fall under the rubric of academic freedom, since it is not concerned with advancing and communicating the scholarship of the faculty member. It is better viewed as an example of professors exercising their rights to free speech as private citizens. Even so, universities generally have a stake in accepting the notion that professors will sometimes play a visible role in the public sphere.

Early on, the AAUP objected that disciplining faculty members for the arguments that they made in the public sphere could easily become the backdoor means for punishing them for their core professional duties as teachers and researchers. Moreover, if university officials were to patrol extramural speech and punish faculty members who stepped out of line, then it would effectively say to members of the faculty that they "cannot afford the luxury of ranging thought and bold speech. Our campuses would then lose the stimulus of clashing opinions and would become havens of cautious mediocrity."[166] A campus that shunned members of its faculty for what and how they communicated to the general public was a campus that would become dedicated to breeding only orthodoxy and conformity. While professors have a responsibility to uphold professional standards when testifying at a legislative hearing or writing in a newspaper on matters within their scholarly expertise, just as they do when publishing an academic monograph or lecturing to a classroom, they should have the freedom to speak their mind in the civic sphere. A campus that could not tolerate differences of opinion on political, religious, or social questions could hardly be expected to create an environment in which scholars could unflinchingly pursue the truth and hold up accepted wisdom to skeptical scrutiny.

The extramural speech of professors is perhaps more visible than it has ever been before. Public speeches might be recorded and made visible to a vastly wider audience on YouTube. An op-ed need not be offered to a newspaper editor when it can be posted on a blog. A conversation that might once have been restricted to the back table in a local bar can now be reduced to 140 characters and posted online. An online "watchlist" of controversial professors can assemble information that might previously have been widely dispersed, and bring it to an audience that is motivated to care and respond to it, even if they had no previous interest in or knowledge of the professors in question, their work, or their home institutions.

The basic principle that faculty members should be free to be engaged citizens and that campuses should be sanctuaries for heterodox views remains true, but the furor that can be ignited by extramural speech has only intensified. The Kansas Board of Regents amply illustrated the dangers in 2014 when it adopted a policy authorizing university presidents to terminate tenured faculty members for "improper use of social media," which was understood to include communications that university administrators deemed "contrary to the best interests of the University." The new policy was adopted after the regents grew frustrated that it was not possible to fire a tenured journalism professor who posted a tweet saying that "blood is on the hands" of the National Rifle Association after a civilian contractor shot a dozen people at the Washington Navy Yard. Indeed, the dean of the Kansas journalism school had already suspended the journalism professor, arguing that his First Amendment rights to free speech "must be balanced with the rights of others," while Kansas political leaders and the National Rifle Association called for him to be fired. Unsurprisingly, academics thought the new social media policy was deeply at odds with the principles of free speech on campus. As one political scientist noted, it would be easy to imagine that a blog post about her current research on same-sex marriage could be regarded as "contrary to the best interests of the University" by regents who had at that time been appointed by a Kansas governor who was leading the charge against same-sex marriage.[167] There is no clear divide between extramural speech and the core scholarly work of academics, and policies designed to restrict the former will inevitably affect the latter.

Professors are hardly unique in being exposed to the ill humors of Internet mobs or discovering that an incautious post on social media has angered their employers. Professors are more distinctive in the role that they occupy within universities. Where a corporation might be quick to cut ties with an employee involved in a scandal that might damage the corporation's own public image or cost it business, the central commitment of the idea of academic freedom is that the relationship between universities and their faculty does not mirror the usual relationship between employer and employee. It should be understood that individual faculty members do not speak for or represent the institution. Rather, the institution houses dozens or hundreds of diverse and conflicting faculty members. The "brand" to be protected in the case of the university should be the one reflected in its institutional mission of facilitating the pursuit of knowledge through vigorous debate and open inquiry. The presence of unorthodox, controversial, and even wild-eyed professors on the faculty should be regarded as a sign of institutional health. The far larger threat to the reputation of a university should be the stifling docility of "cautious mediocrity" or the unimaginative regimentation of ideological conformity.

In recent years, there has been a steady parade of professors getting into hot water because of extramural speech. Sometimes, institutions have stood up for the freedom of individual faculty members to say and do controversial, offensive, and wrongheaded things, but they not infrequently fail to respect or defend basic commitments to academic freedom. The pressure to cave in to demands that the university excise a scandalous member of the faculty is often intense. A necessary step toward resisting such demands is an appreciation of what the mission of a university is, and how a robust commitment to freedom of speech is necessary to that mission.

On occasion, those principles are reaffirmed by universities that find themselves embroiled in public scandal. The University of British Columbia (UBC) in Canada has entered into a collective bargaining agreement with its faculty that recognizes that the two "essential functions" of the university are the production and dissemination of knowledge, and that includes a robust recognition of the principles of academic freedom. In 2015, a business school professor of leadership studies, Jennifer Berdahl, published a blog post commenting on the resignation of UBC president Arvind Gupta as an example of the struggle faced by minorities in leadership positions. She soon received a phone call from the chairman of the governing board of UBC taking her to task for the public post, which was followed by business school officials chastising her for irritating a major donor to the school and discouraging her from publicly expressing any further views about UBC leadership. She instead publicized the effort to silence her. To its credit, the university community rallied around Berdahl, and financier John Montalbano resigned from his position as chairman of the UBC board of governors.[168] Montalbano took the view that professors, as employees of the institution, had a responsibility to refrain from stirring up controversy about the internal workings of the university or criticizing the decisions of its leadership. Such a view is radically at odds with the understanding of the role of the faculty in a university that had been developed over the course of the twentieth century. When the chairman of the board of governors failed to appreciate and defend those principles of academic freedom, his role within the university became untenable.

Universities do not always rise to the challenge when their core principles are tested. The year before the events at UBC, the University of Illinois at Urbana-Champaign faced an even more high-profile and protracted crisis and did not behave so well. The university extended a tenured offer to Steven Salaita, who was then teaching in the English department at Virginia Tech University, to join the faculty of the American Indian studies program at Illinois. Given that much of his research focused on the contemporary experience of Palestinians and Arabs in the Middle East and the United States, and he was politically outspoken on related issues, he had already generated some controversy at Virginia Tech. A large number of faculty members objected when Virginia Tech issued a statement strongly distancing "the greater university community" from Salaita's opinions, even while acknowledging that he had the right to express them. The faculty thought the episode reflected the fact that Virginia Tech was "not a hospitable climate for difference."[169] Shortly before Salaita was to begin his new teaching duties at Illinois, Chancellor Phyllis Wise withdrew the offer in light of a new controversy that had emerged over his Twitter postings, some of which were deemed offensive and potentially anti-Semitic.[170] Wise issued a statement defending her actions, arguing that the university cannot tolerate "personal and disrespectful words or actions that demean and abuse either viewpoints themselves or those who express them," and that faculty had a responsibility in all circumstances to discuss their opinions "in a scholarly, civil and productive manner." Salaita's tweets raised the possibility that some students might not believe that "every instructor recognizes and values that student as a human being." The board of trustees chaired by Christopher Kennedy issued its own statement, declaring that the university "values civility as much as scholarship," and that "disrespectful and demeaning" speech had "no place . . . in our democracy, and therefore, there will be no place for it in our university."[171]

The Salaita affair at the University of Illinois soon became a national controversy in academic circles. There was legal sparring over whether Salaita had been fired or had merely had a "conditional offer" of employment withdrawn before it was ever finalized, but there was no question about the issue of free speech raised by the university's actions. Cary Nelson—proud 1990s "tenured radical," national president of the AAUP in the early 2000s, and chaired professor in the English department at Illinois—became a leading faculty supporter of Wise's action. Nelson tried to toe an artful line between the university administration and its critics by arguing that Salaita's tweets were "loathsome," "inflammatory," "sophomoric and irresponsible," "low comedy," "anti-Semitism," almost maybe incitements to violence, and the "sordid underbelly, the more frank and revealing counterpart" to his scholarly work critiquing Israeli policy regarding the Palestinians, but not actually covered by academic freedom because Salaita's employment contract had not yet been finalized.[172] Critics responded that Nelson was sacrificing long-standing commitments to academic freedom because of his history of disagreement with Salaita over Israeli-Palestinian relations and the appropriate response to that conflict (Salaita is an advocate of American academics boycotting Israeli academic conferences and severing ties with Israeli academics, and Nelson is an opponent of that movement). Even if it were true that Salaita's employment status with the University of Illinois had not yet been finalized, it was contrary to the principles of academic freedom for the university to seek to exclude from its community those who might make "intemperate expressions of opinion on the Israel-Palestine conflict."[173] When the university was forced to divulge its emails relating to the Salaita case, it was evident that the chancellor had initially tried to defend Salaita on academic freedom grounds but reversed course under pressure from donors and the board of trustees, who threatened to cut off support of the university if it did not sever ties with a professor with whom they "vehemently disagree." The chancellor reassured donors that she was busily learning "about Steven Salaita's background, beyond his academic history," and consulted almost exclusively with donors and her public relations and fund-raising staff before deciding to "rescind" Salaita's employment contract.[174] In the face of widespread academic boycotts of the University of Illinois and a series of adverse court rulings, Wise resigned as chancellor and the board of trustees paid Salaita to drop his lawsuit.

The Salaita case attracted extraordinary public attention, but it was only a single skirmish in a long-running battle over the freedom of faculty members to engage in controversial speech. Social media has often been at the center of those battles. No doubt, the very nature of social media platforms like Twitter has a tendency to draw out ill-considered and crudely expressed comments and put them on permanent public display. From there, offhand and out-of-context remarks have the

potential to reach vast unintended audiences, who can be motivated to shine an unwelcome spotlight on an institution. Professors sometimes say foolish things (and, admittedly, "sometimes" might be an understatement), but the consequences of
such missteps can be much greater now than they once were.
Offensiveness can readily become the trigger for the enforcement of ideological and political boundaries on campus.
Sometimes, the offended parties are inside the university, as
was the case with a tenured Marquette University political scientist who published a blog post critical of how a graduate
teaching assistant in the philosophy department had treated an
undergraduate in her class over the student's remarks about
same-sex marriage. His dean swiftly informed him that he
would be stripped of tenure and fired because the blog post
constituted "dishonorable, irresponsible, or incompetent conduct" that had significantly reduced the faculty member's
"value" to the university. The professor was eventually offered
the opportunity to apologize for the blog post, but he refused
and so remained suspended from his duties.[175] At other times,
the offended parties are outside the university, as was the case
with a tenured Drexel University political scientist who posted
tweets fantasizing about "white genocide" and expressing the
desire to "vomit" at the sight of fellow travelers thanking a uni-
formed American soldier for his service. After his tweets were
picked up by the national media, his provost informed him
that his position at the university was "under review" because
his "provocative tweets" had caused "serious damage" to the
university's brand and become a "serious distraction" owing to
the "nearly unmanageable number of venomous calls" to university officials and the fact that "at least two potential significant donors to the university have withheld previously promised donations."[176] In the eyes of some senior university

administrators, academic freedom is all to the good, until it starts affecting fund-raising.

There is no question that in many such cases, the faculty members who find themselves mired in controversy could have behaved better. Scholars who are concerned with improving our understanding of the world have a responsibility to try to shed light on difficult topics, not turn up the heat on emotional brawls. Even so, such missteps should not become the opportunity for administrators to purge universities of quarrelsome faculty. Doing so simply deters other professors from entering public debates, and as a consequence denies the public the benefit of potentially helpful scholarly insights. Moreover, the instances of professors who find themselves engulfed in public firestorms through no fault of their own emphasize the importance of universities tolerating and standing up for their own faculty. Tenured philosophy professor Tommy Curry at Texas A&M University found himself under fire when some conservative publications used out-of-context snippets of a podcast interview in which he discussed race in American history and the recent film *Django Unchained* to portray him as an advocate of racial violence. The university president intervened to denounce Curry's comments as "disturbing" and contrary to "Aggie core values." Meanwhile, the professor was subjected to death threats and vile racial slurs. Only days later did A&M's president begin to backpedal and point out that Curry's views had been misrepresented in the press, and that scholars have a duty to explore difficult arguments even when their work "can be oversimplified and distorted" by outsiders working through sound bites.[177] The point of academic freedom is not to insulate professors from deserved public criticism, but it should protect faculty from reprisals for voicing unpopular opinions. Even more fundamentally, a healthy liberal society in a liberal republic should be capable of tolerating dissenters without subjecting them to anonymous death threats, hateful email, and calls for personal financial ruin.

Securing the conditions under which scholars can freely examine important matters of public concern and reach unpopular conclusions about them requires that leaders in higher education defend the principles of intellectual freedom against those both on and off campus who would seek to curtail such inquiries and insist that academic research only confirm the conventional wisdom. This is a familiar problem of free speech. Even those who have a general commitment to the ideal of free speech can have difficulty adhering to that ideal when confronted with particular examples of speech that they find disturbing or offensive. Elected politicians often find themselves catering to the sensitivities of the voters when faced with unpopular speech, and one of the virtues of a politically insulated judiciary is that judges are more likely to defend for the general principles of free speech and evenhandedly apply them to dissenters. University leaders are not as insulated as judges, but they have a similar responsibility to safeguard the general principles of free speech even when particular instances of speech are distasteful. In protecting the freedom of intellectual inquiry in those shocking instances, universities secure the conditions for probing scholarly investigations more generally.

# Ideological Ostracism
# and Viewpoint Diversity
# on Campus

Universities need not be committed to a mission of advancing and disseminating knowledge. They need not serve as sanctuaries for free inquiry in the search of truth. The University of Notre Dame could declare that it would henceforth refuse to allow scholarly research or teaching on its campus that calls into questions any components of the Catholic faith. Middlebury College could announce that in the future it will allow on campus only discussions that are designed to advance the political commitments favored by its current student body. The University of Illinois could proclaim that it will tolerate on its campus only speech that will give no offense to the elected representatives of the state of Illinois and their agents on the university board of trustees (though the school would run into constitutional constraints on that one).

Few universities in the United States, or indeed in much of the Western world, are willing to make such a public pronouncement. The value of such circumscribed institutions of higher education is limited, and the constituencies interested in supporting such institutions are few. Colleges like Oberlin and Reed would prefer not to give the impression that their faculty and students are required to pledge themselves to a statement of faith in order to remain campus members in good standing. Modern universities instead prefer to advertise themselves as committed to the pursuit of truth rather than to the recitation of dogma. Actually following through on that commitment often proves difficult. Some of those difficulties are theoretical. In order to protect free speech, we must first understand what is required by the principles of free speech. Some of those difficulties are practical. In order to preserve a campus environment that respects free speech, we must be able to resist the constant temptations to suppress the inconvenient, the troublesome, the unpopular, and the offensive. Some of those difficulties are normative. In order to sustain institutions of higher education that contribute to human progress, we must commit ourselves to liberal values of tolerance and freedom rather than to illiberal values of conformity and coercion. It is only by acknowledging those principles of free speech and respecting them, however, that universities are able to realize their promise and make their best contribution to society.

Embracing free speech is easy if the speech never seems very challenging. It is easy to listen to pleasing ideas and affirmations of our own prior beliefs. It is much more difficult to learn to tolerate those with whom we disagree and who espouse ideas we find preposterous, repugnant, or even dangerous. We tolerate, and even affirmatively seek out, such disagreements not because they are pleasant but because it is through controversy that we can make progress, often in the most unexpected ways. At their best, universities tolerate controversies in the hopes that some of those controversies will generate not just heat but light. As students and scholars, we should welcome controversies that test our ideas and speculations and help us discard those arguments that are weak and build on those that are proven strong.

Universities across the country and the world strive to assemble the best community of scholars and students that they can. The members of those communities can boast impressive professional credentials and markers of intellectual achievement, and the competition to join the most selective institutions of higher education can be fierce. Prospective members of the faculty prepare to join those communities not through the rough-and-tumble of John Stuart Mill's debating societies but through the intensive disciplinary training pioneered by the German universities in the late nineteenth century. They are trained to question what we know and push the boundaries of knowledge outward, and they seek to lead classrooms where students can learn to challenge themselves and find their own convictions unsettled.

Unfortunately, universities sometimes struggle to sustain the kind of diverse intellectual communities that would best facilitate the advancement and dissemination of knowledge. Mill worried that a closed society, too comfortable in its own convictions, would retreat into dogmatism. It would not have the opportunity to grapple with diverse opinions, to have its own opinions tested, to refine its own ideas by identifying and shedding those that were weak and borrowing and bolstering those that were strong. Academia values skepticism, not credulity, but that requires bringing to campus those who will question and not merely affirm. Modern academic disciplines make progress by systematically screening out ideas and arguments that cannot survive careful scrutiny. In this way, they insist not on homogeneity but on expertise. They do not require agreement, but they do require competence and mastery of an established body of knowledge and accepted tools for acquiring new knowledge. The university does not need the Young Earth theorist, the flat earth true believer, or the Bigfoot specialist in order to make scientific progress and host serious scientific debate. But if a community of scholars is not to become lethargic, and if the advancement of knowledge is to proceed, scholars cannot become complacent in their studies and blind to their deficiencies and biases.

It is important to emphasize that most scholarly disputes fly far below the public's radar, but that internecine squabbling has large consequences for the future of teaching and research on college campuses. In history departments, traditional political history (which emphasized politicians and public policy) was crowded out by the rise of social history (which emphasized ordinary people and daily life) before making a bit of a comeback in a form that was influenced by the insights of social history. In economics departments, upstart "freshwater" economists based at universities near the Great Lakes disagreed with more traditional "saltwater" economists based at universities on the East Coast over how we should understand the workings of national economies and what public policies might contribute to stable economic growth. In political science departments, the introduction of game theoretic models of political behavior disrupted established ways of thinking, just as the introduction of statistical models had done a generation or two earlier. When most scholars think about intellectual diversity, or its absence, they think about these sorts of esoteric disputes.

We rarely think of these sorts of scholarly disagreements as implicating free speech or academic freedom on campus. In part, that is because scholars are generally committed to engaging openly and aggressively in exactly these sorts of academic debates. To the extent that the fortunes of some schools of thought rise or fall as a consequence of those debates, we recognize those fluctuating fortunes as being the result of professional judgments. If disciplinary judgments on these matters turn out to be wrong, we expect them to be corrected through new rounds of scholarly engagement. Revisionist scholarship upsets the status quo and forces established schools of thought to defend their conclusions anew and adjust to new findings.

It marks a fundamental misunderstanding of academic life to conflate scholarly disagreements and political disagreements. It is perfectly possible for university faculties to overwhelmingly hail from the political left and yet disagree vehemently with one another on matters of scholarship and teaching, and it is likewise possible for faculty members who would be very much at odds with one another in the realm of politics to be in complete agreement in the realm of scholarship. Only someone who does not understand what happens on college campuses could declare, as the office of US Senator Tom Coburn did, that "political science would be better left to pundits and voters," or that "CNN, Fox News, MSNBC, the print media, and a seemingly endless number of political commentators on the internet" serve the same function as the venerable American National Election Studies of public opinion managed by the University of Michigan and Stanford

University.[1] Pundits on CNN and political scientists in their ivory tower both have their contributions to make to society, but it is a fundamental error to think that those contributions are of the same type and one or the other is simply redundant.

Unfortunately, some members of the campus community seem similarly confused, and therein lies the problem for those concerned about intellectual diversity and free speech on college campuses. The evidence that American university faculties lean to the left in their political preferences is overwhelming. While the gap is smaller in some disciplines (e.g., engineering), it is extremely large in many others (e.g., sociology).[2] It would be a reasonable, and in many ways correct, response to this fact to say that for most purposes the political preferences of university faculty members have nothing to do with their work and how they conduct it. It is much less reasonable to respond, as many academics have, that university faculties *should* lean to the left. When the chair of a philosophy department says that the empirical finding that university faculties include few conservatives is unsurprising because "stupid people are generally conservative"; when an English professor declares "colleges and universities do not need a single additional 'conservative' . . . what they do need, and would much benefit from, is more Marxists, radicals, leftists—all terms conventionally applied to those who fight against exploitation, racism, sexism, and capitalism"; and when a soon-to-be law school dean observes that conservatives are adequately represented in elected offices and thus have no claim to being "an embattled minority" in the groves of academe—one then suspects that the diversity of thought on campus is inadequate.[3]

We should take into account this context when considering, in particular, the controversies that have surrounded invitations to campus speakers. When few conservative faculty members can be found on a college campus, students and others seeking to hear a conservative perspective on matters of public concern by necessity must look beyond campus. Preferably, the goal of such invitations should not be to replicate what could easily be found by simply turning on a cable news show. It is to be hoped that any speaker invited to a college campus can provide a more extended and more serious analysis of topics than might be covered in the mainstream press, and even better could explore ideas and issues that are not sufficiently discussed in other venues. It is a missed opportunity if time, resources, and energy are committed to hosting events that do not advance the distinctive mission of a university and aspirations of a campus community, but are instead spent facilitating the business of professional agitators.

Obstructions of campus speakers have the immediate effect of preventing a willing audience from hearing the arguments that the speaker was invited to convey, but obstructionist protest tactics have an additional effect as well. They are efforts not merely to shout down a particular speech, but to ostracize the speaker from the campus community. They are designed not only to prevent a particular message from being heard, but also to send a message of their own: you will not be tolerated here. The censors of yore punished speakers for what they said and prevented publication of writings that contained controversial content. Obstructionist protesters, by contrast, do not wait to hear the speech before deciding whether it should be suppressed. They engage in suppression before the content of the message is even known. The protesters object to the very presence of an Ann Coulter or a Charles Murray on campus.

The Charles Murray fracas at Middlebury College made the goal of ideological ostracism plain. Murray was invited to speak in 2017 about a topic related to his most recent book on class, culture, and polarization in contemporary American life. He was pilloried for arguments he had made in *The Bell Curve*, a controversial book he wrote more than two decades earlier and before many of the undergraduates at Middlebury had even been born. Even so, many of the members of Middlebury's faculty who signed a letter denouncing his appearance on campus admitted that they had never actually read anything that Murray had written but had simply been told that he was a "white nationalist." When a team of psychologists sent a blind copy of a transcript of Murray's remarks to a sample of college professors and asked them to rate its content on a left–right ideological spectrum, they rated it as "middle of the road." (When a second sample was told the name of the author, they gave it a substantially more conservative rating but still near the middle of the scale.)[4] The obstruction of Murray's speech was an effort to enforce ideological boundaries on Middlebury's campus by ostracizing anyone who might be thought to hold problematic views. To complete that effort, the chairman of the department that cosponsored Murray's talk was forced to issue a public apology for his role in breaking campus taboos and bringing a forbidden person to campus.[5]

A similar effort to purge the campus of the unclean took place a few years earlier at the University of California at Berkeley. John Yoo is a tenured conservative law professor and served in the Office of Legal Counsel in the Department of Justice under President George W. Bush. As with many university professors who have taken a leave of absence to spend time in public service, Yoo returned to campus after his brief stint in the government. Yoo's situation was unusual, however, in that it was soon revealed that he had drafted controversial opinions justifying the administration's legal position in the early days of the War on Terror after the attacks on September 11, 2001. In particular, he had authored what was dubbed the "torture memo," subsequently rescinded, that provided legal cover for so-called enhanced interrogation of captured suspected terrorists. As a result of his actions in the government, many on the Berkeley campus called for him to be fired from his job at the law school. An email campaign argued that Yoo "should be prohibited from spreading his distorted view of the law and the role of lawyers to young law students. He must be fired."[6] To the consternation of critics, the dean of Berkeley's law school maintained that absent a showing of professional misconduct or criminal behavior by Yoo, he was not "beyond the pale of academic freedom." Berkeley's law school was to be a place where faculty and students could argue "about the legal and moral issues with the intensity and discipline these crucial issues deserve." Those who were unwilling to face up to the ideas that they would condemn, and would prefer to avoid controversial arguments rather than grappling with them, "will not find Berkeley or any other truly great law school a wholly congenial place to study."[7] Yoo is one of the very few conservative members of the Berkeley law school faculty, his scholarship is prominent within his field of expertise, and his views of the legal issues surrounding the War on Terror remain an important part of the public debate. His removal from campus would significantly reduce the range of perspectives and the scope of arguments that students at Berkeley would be likely to encounter, much to the detriment of the quality of their legal education. As the left-leaning legal theorist Brian Leiter argued at the time, Yoo's views as reflected in his OLC memos and elsewhere might be "implausible, badly argued and morally odious," but if that were sufficient to warrant removing a tenured faculty member for research misconduct, then "there would be nothing left of academic freedom, since every disagreement on the merits of a position, especially a minority position in the scholarly community, could be turned into a 'research misconduct' charge that would lead to disciplinary proceedings and possible termination."[8]

Conservatives are not the only targets of ideological purges in contemporary academia. To take a recent example, the philosopher Rebecca Tuvel published an article in the interdisciplinary feminist philosophy journal *Hypatia* examining the conceptual linkages between "transgenderism" and "transracialism." Upon its publication, a group of associate editors for the journal issued a public letter of "apology . . . for the harms that the publication of the article on transracialism has caused," and exclaimed that "the article should not have been published." The associate editors pledged to consider retracting the article, but they drew a line at outing the anonymous peer reviewers who played a role in moving the article toward publication.[9] An "open letter" was promptly circulated among hundreds of feminist scholars calling on the journal to immediately retract the article since "its continued availability causes further harm," and demanding that any manuscripts on such topics in the future be reviewed by "referees working in critical race theory and trans theory," who could have been expected to spike the offending article before publication.[10] Deploying the tropes used to suppress "hate speech," one widely circulated critique accused Tuvel of engaging in "discursive transmisogynistic violence" and observed that "cis women enacting violence against women of color is not the exception; it is the rule," though its author later explained that outsiders did not have the "conceptual competence" to understand what she meant by "violence."[11] Tuvel's dissertation adviser revealed that though some critics admitted that they had not read the article in question and others privately expressed their sympathy with Tuvel, they all felt obliged to publicly denounce her for her sins lest their own careers also be put in jeopardy.[12] The reaction beyond the feminist community was swift. The attacks on Tuvel were a "witch-hunt," "innuendo [and] name-calling," "defamation" of the professional competence of a junior scholar, and the work of "feminist thought police."[13] Philosophers at large wondered whether the feminist scholars engaged in the attack on Tuvel were practicing philosophy at all or had rather made a profession out of political activism and indoctrination, since they seemed committed to the view that some questions could not be asked, and some conclusions could not be stated if they were intellectually true but politically unpalatable. Eventually the *Hypatia* editor tried to salvage her journal's reputation by denouncing the associate editors for acting in a way that was "utterly inappropriate" in attempting to "repudiate" an article that their journal had published after its normal process of peer review, an article that was professionally sound.[14]

Even more disturbing has been the recent uptick of threats of violence against professors who step out of line on American university campuses. There was a swift retraction of an article published in a political science journal arguing that imperialism had more beneficial aspects for native populations in colonized territories than was often appreciated. The article might well have been wrong or badly argued, and some initial calls for retraction were based simply on those sorts of substantive disagreements with the work, the kind of substantive disagreements that are better vetted through rejoinders than through petitions. The quick decision to send the offending academic article down the memory hole, however, was made by the publisher in the face of what it called "serious and credible threats of personal violence" directed at the journal editor.[15] Similarly, Drexel University decided once again to suspend its most notorious professor over tweets about the Las Vegas mass shooting in October 2017. Because of "a growing number of threats" directed at the professor, the "safety of our campus" had to take priority over free speech and the professor had to be removed.[16] Evergreen College likewise appealed to campus safety as the reason for suspending a professor who came under fire from students for questioning a proposed "Day of Absence" on which white students and faculty were asked to stay away from campus.[17]

Such purges are not designed to filter out would-be scholars who do not meet professional standards nor to dedicate intellectual energy to the most promising lines of scholarly inquiry. They are designed to impose and enforce ideological boundaries on the scope of academic discussion. Ideas without any credible intellectual grounding can be ignored. Arguments that are simply mistaken can be corrected through further argumentation and research. Scholars who have engaged in misconduct can be exposed and disciplined through fair procedures. Speakers who say what may not be said should not simply be excluded, and professors who step outside the bounds of academic or societal orthodoxy should not be threatened with violence or termination.

While such episodes might showcase academic communities that are failing to live up to their own ideals, do they actually pose a problem for the mission of a university? If the artificial constraints on the intellectual diversity tolerated on campus had no real consequences for the pursuit of truth or the advancement and dissemination of knowledge, then those constraints might be annoying and embarrassing but of no great significance.

It seems naive to imagine that such might be the case. Certainly in other contexts, we tend to think that artificial boundaries on the pursuit of knowledge and exclusions from the scholarly community are damaging not only to those left on the outside but also to those within the community. As Mill pointed out, it is the closed society that will not hear from outsiders that suffers the most from the intellectual blinders it has imposed on itself. Ignorance flourishes where free inquiry is impeded. Flawed assumptions go unchallenged. Weak arguments go uncorrected. The agenda for intellectual investigation itself is restricted as questions go unasked. Indeed, part of the rationale for adding gender, racial, and global diversity to American college campuses is that individuals with different experiences and perspectives will improve the quality of academic discourse. Specifically ignoring the value of nurturing greater intellectual diversity on campus seems misguided.

American law schools can provide one particular example of these difficulties. Unlike, say, English departments, law schools have an ongoing connection to the wider world beyond campus since it is central to their particular mission to produce lawyers capable of successfully arguing cases before a range of judges, to work with government officials to reform and apply the law, and to generate research relevant to practicing legal professionals. Unlike, say, engineering schools, law schools provide professional training that is deeply intertwined with controversial ideas about politics and society. It is therefore striking that the political orientation of law schools is closer to that of English departments than to that of engineering schools. Whether measured by self-identification, voter registration, or campaign donations, the faculty members of American law schools lean heavily toward the political left and the Democratic Party.[18] Moreover, they lean much further to the left than does the general population of lawyers in the country, and they include a far smaller proportion of conservatives or Republicans. In short, the political and ideological commitments of law school faculty members much more closely resemble those of university faculty generally than those of the legal profession generally.[19]

Should we have any concerns about that sort of ideological homogeneity in the law schools? Perhaps some. An important part of the teaching and research of a law school involves hands-on engagement with the practice of law, including litigation. Thus Yale Law School celebrates its partnership with the San Francisco city attorney in which its students gained experience working on the federal lawsuit seeking to strike down President Trump's executive order on sanctuary cities.[20] Berkeley's Death Penalty Clinic takes a "social justice orientation" to representing death row prisoners in appealing their convictions and sentences.[21] Such programs are vital, if sometimes controversial, components of modern American law schools, but they also have systematic political and social consequences. If students could benefit from hands-on experience in civil rights, social justice, and environmental litigation, then surely they could likewise benefit from the opportunity to do the kind of work favored by the libertarian public interest law firm Institute for Justice or the conservative Becket Fund for Religious Liberty.

More generally, law professors provide the intellectual resources for legal innovation through their research, teaching, and advocacy. With Ronald Reagan in the White House in the early 1980s, groups of conservative students at a set of elite schools organized themselves to host conferences that could bring some conservative lawyers to speak on important legal issues and debate their liberal law professors. From those efforts, the Federalist Society was born as a conservative "counter-network" to the well-established "liberal legal network" that connected law schools to liberal legal interest groups and Democratic government officials. In the years since, the Federalist Society has made little impact on the composition of law school faculties but has instead become a debating society that intersects with but operates outside of the law schools, and an alternative source of legal ideas for conservative litigators and judges.[22] A group of conservative and libertarian law professors has recently proposed that the Association of American Law Schools approach "viewpoint or political diversity" as it has gender and racial diversity and examine how it organizes its own scholarly conferences, and how law schools treat their individual faculties, though to little immediate effect.[23] For most law professors, many of the landmark constitutional decisions handed down by the conservative justices of the Rehnquist and Roberts courts were both unexpected and almost literally incomprehensible. They reflected the ideas that had been incubated within the alternative intellectual space of the Federalist Society, just as the opinions handed down by the more left-leaning members of the court expressed ideas that had been gestated within the law schools. Law students are underserved if they are exposed to only one side of the intellectual forces that are shaping American law, and all sides within the intellectual debate suffer if they segregate themselves from their opponents rather than engage them.

The lack of viewpoint diversity on campus has also encouraged political backlash.[24] Although the economic, social, and cultural value of universities should encourage their broad support, it has become too easy for some to conclude that they have no stake in the success of universities. Both conservative professors and conservative students often find themselves beleaguered on campus.[25] Conservative interest groups have fanned the flames of mass resentment of the universities.[26] Conservative voters, politicians, and alumni are increasingly adopting the view that mainstream colleges and universities are agents of left-wing politics that should be starved or dismantled. If university faculty understand themselves to be a force of progressive social and political change, it should not be surprising if conservatives use the tools at their disposal to fight back.

It would be preferable if the future of universities did not devolve into a partisan battle. A sincere commitment to preserving free speech on campus and sustaining a space for diverse intellectual arguments is an essential element of demonstrating the value of universities to a broad constituency. Legislative or alumni interventions into campus affairs with a goal of tilting the ideological balance in universities are often clumsy and ham-handed. They subvert important safeguards of university autonomy and intellectual experimentation and distort academic endeavors. The pressure for such outside interventions will only intensify, however, if universities do not seem to be keeping their own house in order. If universities position themselves as little more than partisan think tanks or advocates within the culture war, then partisans on the other side will be inclined to treat them as adversaries to be neutered or destroyed.

Outsiders can worry too much about ideological intolerance on college campuses. While disruptive protests are unfortunate and too common, they do not characterize the everyday routine of campus life. In a nation with hundreds of colleges and millions of students, even a daily episode of uncivil behavior would represent but a drop in the sea. The occasional instance of a speaker being shouted down or a class being disrupted commands attention, but such instances tend to overshadow the thousands of campus speakers whose biggest problem is convincing an audience to attend the lecture or the thousands of classroom teachers who are most concerned that students read their assignments and pay attention in class. Those who worry about systematic ideological indoctrination in college classrooms should be heartened by the evidence that students who are most engaged with their professors and their academic work are the least likely to drift to intellectual and political extremes.[27] It is tempting to indulge ourselves and wallow in the examples of campus misbehavior that conform to familiar narratives, but we should be careful not to let such examples overwhelm us. There are troubling currents swirling through college campuses, and there are genuine disagreements about the proper mission of the university and the modes of realizing it, but campuses are not yet in crisis. Colleges do not need to be dismembered or salvaged. They do need to give attention to their foundations, however. The principles of intellectual inquiry and the conditions that sustain it need to be reaffirmed if universities are to remain vibrant and valuable institutions.

The causes of the ideological tilt on college campuses are myriad. Although it might be the case that simple ideological bias sometimes plays a role in faculty hiring, it is probably more common that ideological blinders help shape an academic culture that is inhospitable to dissenting ideas and points of view. It would seem unwise and likely futile to pursue a system of quotas for achieving greater intellectual diversity on campus. The goal should not be to put a thumb on the scale of scholarly merit. Universities must continue to strive to be the best at what they do by cultivating free intellectual inquiry and creative thinking about ideas. Members of the campus community should pause, however, before dismissing the need for intellectual diversity within academia. Those who are tempted to think that conservatives are simply too "stupid" to participate in the scholarly endeavor, or believe that the intellectual contribution of a conservative scholar on campus would be no different from what could be found on a typical evening on Fox News, should pause to consider whether they have retreated too far into an ideological bubble of their own. Nurturing and grappling with dissenting voices within academia would be likely to pay unexpected intellectual dividends as the scope of academic research is expanded, and the representation of thoughtful conservative scholars and teachers on college campuses is likely to encourage greater tolerance, engagement, and dialogue on campus and beyond.

Members of the campus community have a choice to make. The choice before them is hardly new, and is unlikely ever to be resolved once and for all, but it is a choice that is basic to the life of a modern university. They must decide whether they are committed to a joint project of learning and the principles and practices that make learning possible. If universities are to operate at the outer boundaries of our state of knowledge and to push those boundaries further outward, they must be places where new, unorthodox, controversial, and disturbing ideas can be raised and scrutinized. If students are to prepare themselves to critically engage the wide range of perspectives and problems that they will encounter out in the world across their lifetimes, they must learn to grapple with and critically examine ideas they find difficult and offensive. For more than a century, universities have been committed to the mission of advancing and disseminating knowledge, and have recognized that the free-ranging exchange of ideas is essential to the realization of that mission. They have often pursued that mission imperfectly, and they have sometimes needed to be called to account to better appreciate and work to realize their own ideals. Recognizing and respecting the principles of free speech is difficult and challenging, but there is no alternative if we are dedicated to the pursuit of truth. And the pursuit of truth is the noble and important mission of the modern university.

# NOTES

## Preface

1. For a particularly gloomy assessment, see Roberto Stefan Foa and Yascha Mounk, "The Democratic Disconnect," *Journal of Democracy* 27:3 (2016): 5; Roberto Stefan Foa and Yascha Mounk, "The Signs of Deconsolidation," *Journal of Democracy* 28:1 (2017): 5. For a less pessimistic take, see Erik Voeten, "Are People Really Turning Away from Democracy?," *Journal of Democracy* Web Exchange (2017); Pippa Norris, "Is Western Democracy Backsliding? Diagnosing the Risks," *Journal of Democracy* Web Exchange (2017) (http://journalofdemocracy.org/online-exchange-"democratic -deconsolidation").

2. Herbert McClosky and Alida Brill, *Dimensions of Tolerance* (New York: Russell Sage Foundation, 1983), 56.

3. James L. Gibson and Richard D. Bingham, "On the Conceptualization and Measurement of Political Tolerance," *American Political Science Review* 76 (1982): 608.

4. Samuel A. Stouffer, *Communism, Conformity, and Civil Liberties* (Garden City, NY: Doubleday, 1955); John L. Sullivan, James E. Piereson, and George E. Marcus, *Political Tolerance and American Democracy* (Chicago: University of Chicago Press, 1982); James L. Gibson, "Intolerance and Political Repression in the United States: A Half Century after McCarthyism," *American Journal of Political Science* 52 (2008): 96.

5. Kelsey Ann Naughton, Nikki Eastman, and Nico Perrino, *Speaking Freely: What Students Think about Expression at American Colleges* (Philadelphia: Foundation for Individual Rights in Education, 2017). See also Gallup, *Free Expression on Campus: A Survey of U.S. College Students and U.S. Adults* (Washington, DC: Gallup, 2016).

6. James Madison, "To Thomas Jefferson, Oct. 17, 1788," in *The Writings of James Madison*, ed. Gaillard Hunt, vol. 5 (New York: G. P. Putnam's Sons, 1904), 273. Jefferson was thrilled by Madison's conversion to the cause, and quickly agreed with him that the chief danger to liberty in the near term was likely to come from legislatures. "The rising race are all republicans." The tyranny of the executive "will come in its turn; but it will be at a remote period." The American people who emerged from the Revolution knew enough to distrust the executive, but they needed more reminders that elected legislatures could be oppressive as well. Thomas Jefferson, "To James Madison, March 15, 1789," in *The Writings of Thomas Jefferson*, ed. H. A. Washington, vol. 3 (Washington, DC: Taylor & Maury, 1853), 5.

## Introduction

1. "Mrs. Nation Not a Welcome Guest," *San Francisco Chronicle* (March 4, 1903), 7; "Bar Carrie from Campus," *San Francisco Chronicle* (March 6, 1903), 7; "Students Steal Mrs. Nation's Hat," *San Francisco Chronicle* (March 7, 1903), 7.

2. Unruly behavior was hardly unknown on college campuses in the early twentieth century. For example, Berkeley was in a "state of insurrection" in the fall of 1904 when the upperclassmen objected to the efforts of an instructor in military science to instill a bit of military discipline in his cadets, and the faculty chair of the student affairs committee was sent out to threaten the miscreants with expulsion as they pelted him with clods of grass. The students of Franklin & Marshall College burned a professor in effigy for having disciplined two of the members of the baseball team, causing them to miss games. One day in February 1901 the newswires carried not one but two stories of college presidents forced to call in local law enforcement to quell rioting freshmen on campus. "Students Riot over an Order," *San Francisco Chronicle* (November 3, 1904), 1; "Students Burn Professor's Effigy," *Philadelphia Inquirer* (April 10, 1900), 4; "Class Riot at Monmouth," *Chicago Daily Tribune* (February 26, 1901), 4.

3. Werner Lorenz, "Ernst J. Cohn," in *Jurists Uprooted*, ed. Jack Beatson and Reinhard Zimmermann (Oxford: Oxford University Press, 2004); "Restores Professor Attacked by Nazis," *New York Times* (January 15, 1933), 15; "Breslau Students Firm on Ban on Cohn," *New York Times* (January 21, 1933), 7; "Breslau Expects Row on Cohn Today," *New York Times* (January 24, 1933), 11; "Riots in Breslau as Cohn Returns," *New York Times* (January 25, 1933), 6; "Guard Withdrawn, Cohn Drops Classes," *New York Times* (February 2, 1933), 12; "Nazi Clouds over German Universities," *New York Times* (March 26, 1933), SM3; "Prussia Dismisses Jewish Educators," *New York Times* (April 14, 1933), 1.

4. Paul Horwitz, *First Amendment Institutions* (Cambridge, MA: Harvard University Press, 2013), 107.

5. "Free Speech Is Not Violated at Wellesley," *Wellesley News* (April 12, 2017).

## Chapter 1. The Mission of a University

1. Richard Hofstadter, *Anti-Intellectualism in American Life* (New York: Vintage, 1963), 4.

2. Samuel Butler, *The Note-Books of Samuel Butler*, ed. Henry Festing Jones (New York: E. P. Dutton & Co., 1917), 179.

3. Henry Adams, *The Education of Henry Adams* (Boston: Houghton Mifflin Company, 1918), 57.

4. Paul Elmer More, *A New England Group and Others* (Boston: Houghton Mifflin Company, 1921), 8.

5. Richard M. Weaver, *In Defense of Tradition* (Indianapolis, IN: Liberty Fund, 2000), 37.

6. "Sharp Partisan Divisions in Views of National Institutions," Pew Research

Center (July 10, 2017) (http://www.people-press.org/2017/07/10/sharp-partisan
-divisions-in-views-of-national-institutions/).

7. See Sandy Baum, "Higher Education Earnings Premium: Value, Variation, and
Trends," Urban Institute, 2014; Kartik Athreya and Janice Eberly, "Risk, the College
Premium, and Aggregate Human Capital Investment," Richmond Federal Reserve
Bank of Richmond Working Paper 13-02R (2016); Mary C. Daly and Leila Bengali, "Is
It Still Worth Going to College?" Federal Reserve Bank of San Francisco Economic
Letter 2014-13 (2014).

8. Truman J. Backus, "Abstract of a Paper on 'The Philosophy of the College Curriculum,'" *Proceedings of the Twenty-First Convocation of the University of the State of
New York* (Albany, NY: Weed, Parsons & Company, 1884), 205.

9. Thomas Nelson Haskell, *Collegiate Education in Colorado* (Denver, CO: Tribune Steam Book and Job Printing House, 1874), 5.

10. Quoted in Laurence R. Veysey, *The Emergence of the American University* (Chicago: University of Chicago Press, 1965), 14. Some contemporary corporate titans
echo Carnegie's assessment of the value of a college education. Beth McMurtrie, "The
Rich Man's Dropout Club," *Chronicle of Higher Education* (February 8, 2015).

11. Andrew S. Draper, quoted in Veysey, *Emergence of the American University*, 64.

12. James Burrill Angell, "Inaugural Address, University of Michigan, 1871," in
*Selected Addresses* (New York: Longmans, Green, and Co., 1912), 30–31.

13. Raymond S. Tompkins, "Twelve Decline Their Degrees from Amherst," *Baltimore Sun* (June 21, 1923), 1.

14. "U.S. Secretary of Education Betsy DeVos' Prepared Remarks at the 2017
Conservative Political Action Conference," February 23, 2017 (https://www.ed.gov
/news/speeches/us-secretary-education-betsy-devos%E2%80%99-prepared-remarks
-2017-conservative-political-action-conference).

15. William F. Buckley, *God and Man at Yale* (Chicago: Henry Regnery Company,
1951), xvii, xviii.

16. Herbert Marcuse, "Repressive Tolerance," in *A Critique of Pure Tolerance*
(Boston: Beacon Press, 1969), 94.

17. Ibid., 85.

18. Ibid., 101.

19. Ibid., 110, 118.

20. Ibid., 123.

21. Brian Leiter, "Justifying Academic Freedom: Mill and Marcuse Revisited,"
Social Science Research Network (June 3, 2017).

22. The phrase is from Roger Kimball, *Tenured Radicals* (New York: Harper &
Row, 1990). Before becoming president of the American Association of University
Professors, Cary Nelson issued his "manifesto of a tenured radical" in which he elaborated on his "progressive pedagogy" and "agenda of discovery and consciousness-
raising" in the classroom, "an agenda determined by my sense of where the country
and the profession were culturally and politically, an agenda shaped by the cultural
work I thought it was most useful for me to do as a teacher." Such a stance of "un-

ashamed advocacy" in university teaching may or may not make for an interesting classroom experience, but it provides a rather precarious perch from which to urge the voters and taxpayers of the state of Illinois to preserve Professor Nelson's freedom to do so. Cary Nelson, *Manifesto of a Tenured Radical* (New York: New York University Press, 1997), 79–80.

23. Campus Compact, "Presidents' Declaration on the Civil Responsibility of Higher Education" (https://compact.org/resources-for-presidents/presidents-dec laration-on-the-civic-responsibility-of-higher-education/).

24. Robert Maynard Hutchinson, *Great Books: The Foundation of a Liberal Education* (New York: Simon and Schuster, 1954), 23.

25. Gregory Jay and Sandra E. Jones, "The Grassroots Approach to Curriculum Reform: The Cultures and Communities Program," in *Creating a New Kind of University*, ed. Stephen L. Percy, Nancy L. Zimpher, and Mary Jane Brukardt (Bolton, MA: Anker Publishing Company, 2006), 98.

26. Stanley Fish, *Save the World on Your Own Time* (New York: Oxford University Press, 2008).

27. Henry A. Giroux, *Schooling and the Struggle for Public Life* (New York: Taylor & Francis, 2005), 3, 6.

28. Ira Harkavy, "The Role of Universities in Advancing Citizenship and Social Justice in the 21st Century," *Education, Citizenship and Social Justice* 1 (2006): 6.

29. "What Starts Here Changes the World—Place" (2002). (https://www.youtube .com/watch?v=vN5DaivEOuk&index=5&list=PLhpCkvmYnbhDnFyIAWDNDo0 MIcUj9yuRm).

30. Henry A. Giroux, *Neoliberalism's War on Higher Education* (Chicago: Haymarket Books, 2014), 43; Paulo Freire, *Pedagogy of Solidarity* (Walnut Creek, CA: Left Coast Press, 2014), 15; David Randall, *Making Citizens* (New York: National Association of Scholars, 2017), 9.

31. Gregory Bassham, "Mearsheimer's Mistakes: Why Colleges Should (and Inevitably Do) Provide Moral Guidance," *Expositions* 7 (2013): 33; John J. Mearsheimer, "Teaching at the Margins," *Philosophy and Literature* 22 (1998): 195; John J. Mearsheimer, "The Aims of Education," *Philosophy and Literature* 22 (1998): 147.

## Chapter 2. The Tradition of Free Speech

1. On the multiple values advanced by the First Amendment, see Vincent Blasi, "Holmes and the Marketplace of Ideas," *Supreme Court Review 2004* (2005): 1.

2. Rep. John Nicholas, *Annals of Congress*, 5th Cong., 2nd Sess. (July 10, 1798), 2141.

3. Rep. Albert Gallatin, *Annals of Congress*, 5th Cong., 2nd Sess. (July 10, 1798), 2162.

4. Rep. Samuel Dana, *Annals of Congress*, 5th Cong., 2nd Sess. (July 5, 1798), 2112.

5. Rep. John Nicholas, *Annals of Congress*, 5th Cong., 2nd Sess. (July 10, 1798), 2140.

6. *Gazette of the United States* (October 10, 1798), 1.

7. John Cotton, *An Exposition on the 13th Chapter of the Revelation* (London: Livewel Chapman, 1655), 71.

8. John Locke, *A Letter Concerning Toleration* (Indianapolis, IN: Hackett Publishing Co, 1983), 55.

9. John Stuart Mill, *On Liberty, Utilitarianism, and Other Essays* (New York: Oxford University Press, 2015), 7.

10. Ibid., 8.

11. Ibid., 19.

12. Ibid., 20.

13. Ibid., 24.

14. Ibid., 25.

15. Ibid., 33.

16. Ibid., 35–36.

17. Ibid., 34.

18. Ibid., 35.

19. Ibid., 37.

20. Ibid., 42.

21. Ibid., 47.

22. Abrams v. United States, 250 U.S. 616, 630 (1919).

23. John Milton, *Areopagitica and Of Education* (Arlington Heights, IL: AHM Publishing, 1951), 50.

24. For a critique of the workings of the marketplace of ideas, see Stanley Ingber, "The Marketplace of Ideas: A Legitimizing Myth," *Duke Law Journal* 1984 (1984): 1. For a defense in the context of universities, see Christopher T. Wonnell, "Truth and the Marketplace of Ideas," *University of California Davis Law Review* 19 (1986): 669; Joseph Blocher, "Institutions in the Marketplace of Ideas," *Duke Law Journal* 57 (2008): 822.

25. Mill, *On Liberty, Utilitarianism, and Other Essays*, 36.

26. Robert C. Post, *Democracy, Expertise, and Academic Freedom* (New Haven, CT: Yale University Press, 2012).

## Chapter 3. Free Speech on Campus

1. Friedrich Paulsen, *The German Universities and University Study* (New York: Charles Scribner's Sons, 1906), 228, 230, 243, 244.

2. American Association of University Professors, "Report of the Committee of the American Association of University Professors on Academic Freedom and Academic Tenure," *School and Society* 3 (1916): 109, 115, 116.

3. Report of the Committee on Freedom of Expression at Yale, December 23, 1974 (http://yalecollege.yale.edu/deans-office/policies-reports/report-committee-freedom-expression-yale). Notably, a dissenting report was filed by a student member of the committee, who argued that free speech should be suppressed if doing so might

advance the "liberation of all oppressed people and equal opportunities for minority groups."

4. Report of the Committee on Freedom of Expression at the University of Chicago, January 2015 (https://freeexpression.uchicago.edu/sites/freeexpression.uchicago.edu/files/FOECommitteeReport.pdf).

5. Peter Wood, "The University of Chicago's Flawed Support for Freedom of Expression," *Minding the Campus* (October 8, 2015).

6. "Land of the Free?," *Chicago Maroon* (January 9, 2015).

7. James F. Phifer, Krzysztof Z. Kaaniasty, and Fran H. Norris, "The Impact of Natural Disaster on the Health of Older Adults: A Multiwave Perspective," *Journal of Health and Social Behavior* 29 (1988): 75.

8. Allan Young, *The Harmony of Illusions* (Princeton, NJ: Princeton University Press, 1995), 107.

9. For examples of controversies over trigger warnings, see Frank Furedi, *What's Happened to the University?* (New York: Routledge, 2017), 146–166.

10. Colleen Flaherty, "Trigger Unhappy," *Inside Higher Ed* (April 14, 2014).

11. Scott Jaschik, "Flags and Dissent," *Inside Higher Ed* (November 16, 2016).

12. Jess Bidgood, "At Wellesley, Debate over a Statue in Briefs," *New York Times* (February 6, 2014).

13. Network of Women Students Australia, "Trigger Warning Policy" (https://nowsa2017.com/trigger-warning-policy-2/).

14. American Association of University Professors, "On Trigger Warnings" (August 2014) (https://www.aaup.org/report/trigger-warnings).

15. Howard Gillman, Mark A. Graber, and Keith E. Whittington, *American Constitutionalism*, vol. 2 (New York: Oxford University Press, 2013).

16. Michel Foucault, *Discipline and Punish* (New York: Pantheon Books, 1977).

17. "Lehigh Students Study Both Sides of Slavery in Ghana" (https://history.cas2.lehigh.edu/content/lehigh-students-study-both-sides-slavery-ghana).

18. Thomas A. Harris, *I'm OK, You're OK* (New York: Harper & Row, 1969).

19. Paula Rothenberg, "About Racism and Sexism: A Case Study," *Journal of Thought* 20 (1985): 124.

20. Ibid., 125.

21. Estelle B. Freedman, "Small Group Pedagogy: Consciousness Raising in Conservative Times," *NWSA Journal* 2 (1990): 603.

22. Ibid., 609.

23. Ibid.

24. Saundra Gardner, Cynthia Dean, and Deo McKaig, "Responding to Differences in the Classroom: The Politics of Knowledge, Class, and Sexuality," *Sociology of Education* 62 (1989): 66.

25. Na'llah Suad Nasir and Jasiyah Al-Amin, "Creating Identity-Safe Spaces on College Campuses for Muslim Students," *Change* 38 (2006): 22.

26. See, e.g., Paul Hanselman, Sarah K. Bruch, Adam Gamoran, and Geoffrey D. Borman, "Threat in Context: School Moderation of the Impact of Social Identity Threat on Racial/Ethnic Achievement Gaps," *Sociology of Education* 87 (2014): 106;

Mary C. Murphy, Claude M. Steele, and James J. Gross, "Signaling Threat: How Situational Cues Affect Women in Math, Science, and Engineering Settings," *Psychological Science* 18 (2007): 879; Ted Matherly and Anastasiya Pocheptsova Ghosh, "Is What You Feel What They See? Prominent and Subtle Identity Signaling in Intergroup Interactions," *Journal of Behavioral Decision Making* 30 (2017): 828.

27. Lamiya Khandaker, "Why Hate Speech Is Not Free Speech in an 'Inclusive Excellence' Community," *[Connecticut] College Voice* (March 3, 2015).

28. Susan Svrluga, "Someone Wrote 'Trump 2016' on Emory's Campus in Chalk. Some Students Said They No Longer Feel Safe," *Washington Post* (March 24, 2016).

29. Matthew Pratt Guteri, "On Safety and Safe Spaces," *Inside Higher Ed* (August 29, 2016).

30. Ibid.

31. Catherine Piner, "Michigan State Opens a Women-Only Study Space to Men after a Title IX Complaint," *Slate* (July 29, 2016); Michael Levenson, "Harvard Dean Stands Firm against Single-Sex 'Final Clubs,'" *Boston Globe* (February 25, 2017); Zahra S. Hamdani, "Accommodations for Muslim Students at Universities," *University Business* (July/August 2012); Michael Paulson, "Colleges and Evangelicals Collide on Bias Policy," *New York Times* (June 9, 2014).

32. Bill Chappell, "'You Should Be Outraged,' Air Force Academy Head Tells Cadets about Racism on Campus," NPR.org (September 29, 2017) (http://www.npr .org/sections/thetwo-way/2017/09/29/554458065/you-should-be-outraged-air -force-academy-head-tells-cadets-about-racism-on-campu).

33. Ian Dunt, "Union Apologises for Censoring Atheist 'Spaghetti Monster' Poster," Politics.co.uk (February 12, 2014) (http://www.politics.co.uk/news/2014 /02/12/university-apologises-for-censoring-atheist-spaghetti-monste); Hemant Mehta, "London School of Economics Apologizes for Censoring Atheists Who Wore 'Jesus & Mo' Shirts," Patheos.com (December 19, 2013) (http://www.patheos.com /blogs/friendlyatheist/2013/12/19/london-school-of-economics-apologizes-to -atheists-who-wore-jesus-mo-shirts/).

34. Ian Dunt, "Safe Space or Free Speech? The Crisis around Debate at UK Universities," *Guardian* (February 6, 2015) (https://www.theguardian.com/education /2015/feb/06/safe-space-or-free-speech-crisis-debate-uk-universities).

35. Matthew Pratt Guteri, "On Safety and Safe Spaces," *Inside Higher Ed* (August 29, 2016); Robert Boost Rom, "'Safe Spaces': Reflections on an Educational Metaphor," *Journal of Curriculum Studies* 30 (1998): 405.

36. Rom, "'Safe Spaces,'" 406.

37. Ibid., 406, 407.

38. Claire Ballentine, "Freshmen Skipping 'Fun Home' for Moral Reasons," *Duke Chronicle* (August 21, 2015).

39. "A Right to Speak and to Hear: Qur'an Controversy" (http://exhibits.lib.unc .edu/exhibits/show/academic_freedom/summer-readings/quran-controversy).

40. Katherine Farrish, "Dispute over Book Selection Prompts Debate at Connecticut College," *Hartford Courant* (July 12, 1992).

41. John Newsome, "SC Legislators to State Universities: Assign Gay Material, See

Your Money Cut," CNN (March 9, 2014) (http://www.cnn.com/2014/03/09/politics/university-budget-cuts-gay-literature-south-carolina/index.html).

42. Lee C. Bollinger, "Seven Myths about Affirmative Action in Universities," *Willamette Law Review* 38 (2002): 541.

43. American Association of University Professors, "On Trigger Warnings."

44. Ulrich Baer, "What 'Snowflakes' Get Right about Free Speech," *New York Times* (April 24, 2017).

45. Eugene Volokh, "No, Gov. Dean, There Is No 'Hate Speech' Exception to the First Amendment," *Washington Post* (April 21, 2017) (https://www.washingtonpost.com/news/volokh-conspiracy/wp/2017/04/21/no-gov-dean-there-is-no-hate-speech-exception-to-the-first-amendment/?utm_term=.6f73065df031).

46. Kevin Phillips, " 'Hate Speech Is Not Protected by the First Amendment,' Portland Mayor Says. He's Wrong," *Washington Post* (May 30, 2017) (https://www.washingtonpost.com/news/the-fix/wp/2017/05/30/hate-speech-is-not-protected-by-the-first-amendment-oregon-mayor-says-hes-wrong/?utm_term=.af7eb0e53563).

47. Lauren Carroll, "CNN's Chris Cuomo: First Amendment Doesn't Cover Hate Speech," Politifact.com (May 7, 2015) (http://www.politifact.com/punditfact/statements/2015/may/07/chris-cuomo/cnns-chris-cuomo-first-amendment-doesnt-cover-hate/).

48. Jacob Sollum, "Violent Charlottesville Protester Claims 'Free Speech Does Not Protect Hate Speech,' " Reason.com (August 14, 2017) (http://reason.com/blog/2017/08/14/violent-charlottesville-counterprotester).

49. Scott Jaschik, "Study Casts Doubts on Student Support for Free Speech," *Inside Higher Ed* (September 19, 2017) (https://www.insidehighered.com/quicktakes/2017/09/19/study-casts-doubts-student-support-free-speech).

50. Christian Legal Society Chapter of University of California, Hastings College of Law v. Martinez, 130 S.Ct. 2971, 2994n26 (2010).

51. R.A.V. v. St. Paul, 505 U.S. 377, 386 (1992).

52. Virginia v. Black, 538 U.S. 343, 360–361 (2003). See also Watts v. United States, 394 U.S. 705 (1969); Elonis v. United States, 135 S.Ct. 2001 (2015).

53. Matal v. Tam, 137 S.Ct. 1744, 1763 (2017).

54. Whitney v. California, 274 U.S. 357, 371 (1927).

55. "Chiefly about People," *Western Christian Advocate* ( January 28, 1903): 18.

56. Mary Harris Jones, *Autobiography of Mother Jones* (Chicago: Charles H. Kerr & Company, 1925), 145.

57. Chaplinsky v. New Hampshire, 315 U.S. 568, 572 (1942).

58. City of Chicago v. Terminiello, 332 Ill. App. 17, 26, 38, 49 (1947).

59. Terminiello v. Chicago, 337 U.S. 1, 4 (1949).

60. On the spread and persistence of campus speech codes, Jon B. Gould, *Speak No Evil* (Chicago: University of Chicago Press, 2005).

61. Mari J. Matsuda, "Public Response to Racist Speech: Considering the Victim's Story," *Michigan Law Review* 87 (1989): 2357.

62. Lawrence Douglas, "The Force of Words: Fish, Matsuda, MacKinnon, and the Theory of Discursive Violence," *Law and Social Inquiry* 29 (1995): 169.

63. Michel Foucault, *The Archeology of Knowledge and the Discourse on Language* (New York: Pantheon Books, 1972), 229.

64. Bryan Turner, "Obituaries and the Legacy of Derrida," *Theory, Culture & Society* 22 (2005): 132.

65. Patricia Hill Collins, "The Tie That Binds: Race, Gender and US Violence," *Ethnic and Racial Studies* 21 (1998): 923.

66. Bennett Carpenter, "Free Speech, Black Lives and White Fragility," *Duke Chronicle* (January 19, 2016).

67. Lennard Davis, "A Meditation on Violent Language: Professor's Impassioned Tweets vs the University Memo," *Huffington Post* (October 30, 2014).

68. Tyler Gillespie, "How Students Made an Off-Campus Protest a Movement," *Nation* (April 13, 2017).

69. Brad Evans and Henry A. Giroux, "The Violence of Forgetting," *New York Times* (June 20, 2016).

70. Brad Evans and Henry A. Giroux, "Self-Plagiarism and the Politics of Character Assassination: The Case of Zygmunt Bauman," Truthout.org (August 30, 2015) (http://www.truth-out.org/opinion/item/32560-self-plagiarism-and-the-politics-of-character-assassination-the-case-of-zygmunt-bauman?tmpl=component &print=1).

71. Jazz Keyes, "Sticks and Stones: Dismantling Black-on-Black Verbal Violence," *Ebony* (March 21, 2017).

72. Adam Haslett, "Donald Trump, Shamer in Chief," *Nation* (October 4, 2016).

73. Jason Rochlin and Sarah Wolstoncroft, "Republicans at CSUF Accused of Hate Speech for Students for Quality Education Parody Instagram Account," *Daily Titan* (May 7, 2017).

74. Alexander Nazaryan, "White Painter Loses Art Show over Cultural Appropriation Debate," *Newsweek* (May 5, 2017).

75. A Book Named "John Cleland's Memoirs of a Woman of Pleasure" v. Attorney General of Commonwealth of Massachusetts, 383 U.S. 413, 419 (1966).

76. R.A.V. v. City of St. Paul, Minnesota, 505 U.S. 377, 401 (1992).

77. Harry Kalven Jr., "The *New York Times* Case: A Note on the 'Central Meaning of the First Amendment,'" *Supreme Court Review 1964* (1964): 217; Harry Kalven Jr., "The Metaphysics of the Law of Obscenity," *Supreme Court Review 1960* (1960): 11.

78. Cohen v. California, 403 U.S. 15, 26 (1971).

79. Doe v. University of Michigan, 721 F. Supp. 852, 858, 866 (E.D. Mich., 1989).

80. Matsuda, "Public Response to Racist Speech," 2357.

81. https://www.dickinson.edu/download/downloads/id/4882/bias_incident _protocol_2015pdf.pdf

82. "Free Speech University Rankings 2017," Spiked Online (http://www.spiked -online.com/free-speech-university-rankings/results#.WSkd6ty1tdj).

83. Nico Hines, "University College London's Nietzsche Club Is Banned," *Daily Beast* (June 5, 2014) (https://www.thedailybeast.com/university-college-londons -nietzsche-club-is-banned).

84. "LSE Apologises to Students Asked to Cover Jesus and Muhammad T-shirts,"

*Guardian* (December 20, 2013); Lauren Gorton, Charlie Spargo, and Marcus Johns, "*Charlie Hebdo* Cartoon Banned from Refreshers' Fair," *Mancunion* (January 30, 2015).

85. "Pro-Life Group Banned from Scottish University's Freshers' Fair," *Catholic Herald* (September 10, 2014) (http://www.catholicherald.co.uk/news/2014/09/10/pro-life-group-banned-from-scottish-university-freshers-fair/).

86. Matsuda, "Public Response to Racist Speech," 2336, 2360.

87. Alexander Tsesis, *Destructive Messages* (New York: New York University Press, 2002), 136, 173.

88. Shannon Gilreath, " 'Tell Your Faggot Friend He Owes Me $500 for my Broken Hand': Thoughts on a Substantive Equality Theory of Free Speech," *Wake Forest Law Review* 44 (2009): 570.

89. Baer, "What 'Snowflakes' Get Right about Free Speech."

90. Noah Berlatsky, "Why Do Mainstream Pundits Keep Getting Student Protest So Wrong?," *Pacific Standard* (October 11, 2017).

91. Susan Svrluga, "Princeton Protestors: Why We Need Safe Spaces, and Why Honoring Woodrow Wilson Is Spitting in Our Faces," *Washington Post* (December 4, 2015).

92. Quoted in Donald Alexander Downs, *Restoring Free Speech and Liberty on Campus* (New York: Cambridge University Press, 2005), 110.

93. Ruth Serven and Ashley Reese, "In Homecoming Parade, Racial Justice Advocates Take Different Paths," *Columbia Missourian* (October 10, 2015).

94. Claire E. Parker, "Law School Activists Occupy Student Center," *Harvard Crimson* (February 17, 2016).

95. Mary Mogan Edwards, "Occupation Ends at Ohio State University's Bricker Hall after Arrests, Expulsion Threatened," *Columbus Dispatch* (April 7, 2016).

96. Martin Luther King Jr., "Letter from a Birmingham Jail," in Keith E. Whittington, *American Political Thought* (New York: Oxford University Press, 2016), 600.

97. Quoted in Downs, *Restoring Free Speech and Liberty on Campus*, 5.

98. Peter Beinart, "A Violent Attack on Free Speech at Middlebury," *Atlantic* (March 6, 2017).

99. Michael Bodley and Nanette Asimov, "UC Berkeley Cancels Right-Wing Provocateur's Talk amid Violent Protest," *SFGate* (February 2, 2017); Chris Perez and Gina Daldone, "Protesters Storm NYU over Conservative Speaker's Seminar," *New York Post* (February 2, 2017).

100. Emily Fagan and Myles Sauer, "Protesters Crash Effective Altruism Debate," *Martlet* (March 6, 2017); Scott Jaschik, "Who's Intolerant?," *Inside Higher Ed* (December 12, 2016).

101. Samuel Breslow, "Students Blockade Athenaeum to Protest Conservative Speaker," *Student Life* (April 7, 2017).

102. Scott Jaschik, "Anti-Israel Protests Disrupts Film at UC Irvine," *Inside Higher Ed* (May 23, 2016).

103. Eugene Volokh, "UC Santa Barbara Professor Steals Young Anti-Abortion

Protestor's Sign, Apparently Assaults Protestors, Says She 'Set a Good Example for Her Students,'" *Washington Post* (March 20, 2014).

104. Jeremy Bauer-Wolf, "ICE Agent at Northwestern Shut Out of Class," *Inside Higher Ed* (May 18, 2017).

105. Jeremy Bauer-Wolf, "ACLU Speaker Shouted Down at William & Mary, *Inside Higher Ed* (October 5, 2017).

106. Colleen Flaherty, "Classroom, Interrupted," *Inside Higher Ed* (October 11, 2017).

107. Dave Renton, *Fascism, Anti-Fascism, and Britain in the 1940s* (New York: Macmillan Press, 2000), 140–143; Dave Rich, *The Left's Jewish Problem* (London: Biteback Publishing, 2016); Noah Lucas, "Jewish Students, the Jewish Community, and the 'Campus War' in Britain," *Patterns of Prejudice* 19 (1985): 27.

108. "Petition Urges Cardiff University to Cancel Germaine Greer Lecture," *Guardian* (October 23, 2015).

109. Andrew Kugle, "Berkeley Student Arrested after Destroying College Republican Signs," *Washington Free Beacon* (March 6, 2017); Antonella Artuso, "Protesters Crash Controversial U of T Prof's Appearance," *Toronto Sun* (March 17, 2017).

110. Kate Mansfield, "Islamic Society Students Disrupt University Lecture on Blasphemy and Make 'Death Threat,'" *Daily Express* (December 4, 2015).

111. John Patrick Leary, "Bodies on the Gears at Middlebury," *Inside Higher Ed* (March 7, 2017).

112. Linus Owens, Maya Goldberg-Safir, and Rebecca Flores Harper, "Divisiveness Is Not Diversity," *Inside Higher Ed* (March 17, 2017).

113. Ibid.

114. Fagan and Sauer, "Protesters Crash Effective Altruism Debate."

115. Leary, "Bodies on the Gears at Middlebury."

116. See Russel B. Nye, *Fettered Freedom* (Lansing: Michigan State College Press, 1949); Clement Eaton, *The Freedom-of-Thought Struggle in the Old South* (New York: Harper & Row, 1964).

117. Thomas I. Emerson, *The System of Freedom of Expression* (New York: Vintage, 1970), 338.

118. Glasson v. City of Louisville, 518 F.2d 899, 905 (6th Cir., 1975).

119. Terminiello v. City of Chicago, 337 U.S. 4–5 (1949).

120. Monica Wang, Joey Ye, and Victor Wang, "Students Protest Buckley Talk," *Yale Daily News* (November 9, 2015).

121. Josh Logue, "Rush to Revoke (or Not)," *Inside Higher Ed* (October 28, 2015).

122. Philip Rucker and Rosalind S. Helderman, "At Time of Austerity, 8 Universities Spent Top Dollar on Hillary Rodham Clinton Speeches," *Washington Post* ( July 2, 2014); Gromer Jeffers Jr. and Sue Ambrose, "UNT President Opposed Donald Trump Jr.'s $100,000 Speech, but Donors Prevailed," *Dallas Morning News* (October 9, 2017); Claude Brodesser-Akner, "'Snooki' Bill Capping N.J. College Speaking Fees Could Soon Go to Christie," *NJ.com* (March 23, 2017); Jake New, "$135,000 for Commencement Speech?," *Inside Higher Ed* (April 2, 2015).

123. Brian Fraga, "Notre Dame Picks Pence for Commencement Speaker," *National Catholic Register* (March 9, 2017); "After Protest, Jim Webb Declines to Accept Naval Academy Award," *Navy Times* (March 29, 1017); Emma G. Fitzsimmons, "Condoleezza Rice Backs Out of Rutgers Speech after Student Protests," *New York Times* (May 3, 2014); Rosanna Xia, "War Criminal or Role Model? Madeleine Albright as Scripps College Commencement Speaker Hits a Nerve," *Los Angeles Times* (May 9, 2016).

124. Jeremy Bauer-Wolf, "Commencement Controversy of a Different Sort," *Inside Higher Ed* (April 5, 2017); Amanda Hess, "Elite College Students Protest Their Elite Commencement Speakers," *Slate* (May 13, 2014).

125. Heather Schwedel, "Your Definitive Guide to Totally Unobjectionable Commencement Speaker Picks," *Slate* (May 10, 2016); Colleen Flaherty, "Disinvitation Season Begins," *Inside Higher* Ed (February 14, 2017).

126. Harry Enten, "The Disappearance of Conservative Commencement Speakers," *FiveThirtyEight* (May 28, 2014); Michael Gryboski, "Liberals Attempted to Censor College Speakers Twice As Often As Conservatives, Study Finds," *Christian Post* (February 8, 2017); Matt Pearce, "Campus Throwdown: Students Are Forcing Out Graduation Speakers," *Los Angeles Times* (May 15, 2014).

127. Adam Clark, "Steven Van Zandt to Rock Rutgers as 2017 Grad Speaker," *NJ.com* (February 8, 2017).

128. Jordan Sargent, "Big Sean Is Turning Princeton Students into Idiots," *Gawker* (April 29, 2015).

129. Drew Jaffe, "Commencement Speaker Draws Criticism," *Occidental Weekly* (April 26, 2016).

130. Coalition at Oxy for Diversity and Equality, "An Open Letter to Jonathan Veitch," *Facebook* (April 28, 2016) (https://www.facebook.com/permalink.php?story_fbid=1164592903574603&id=626950517338847).

131. Richard Pérez-Peña, "In Season of Protest, Haverford Speaker Is Latest to Bow Out," *New York Times* (May 13, 2014).

132. Susan Snyder, "Haverford College Commencement Speaker Lambastes Students," *Philly.com* (May 18, 2014).

133. Andrew Kreighbaum, "DeVos Booed throughout Speech at Bethune-Cookman," *Inside Higher Ed* (May 10, 2017); "Bethune-Cookman University Graduates 374 Students for Spring Commencement" (http://www.cookman.edu/newsInfo/newsroom/newsReleases/2016/bethune-cookman-university-graduates-374-students-for-spring-commencement.html).

134. Liam Stack, "Notre Dame Students Walk Out of Mike Pence Commencement Address," *New York Times* (May 21, 2017). See also Jacob T. Levy, "Why Walking Out Is Better Than Shouting Down," *Chronicle of Higher Education* (May 25, 2017).

135. Foundation for Individual Rights in Education, "Disinvitation Report 2014: A Disturbing 15-Year Trend" (May 28, 2014) (https://www.thefire.org/disinvitation-season-report-2014/).

136. Healy v. James, 408 U.S. 169, 187, 192, 189 (1972).

137. Rosenberger v. Rector and Visitors of the University of Virginia, 515 U.S. 819, 829 (1995).

138. OSU Student Alliance v. Ray, 699 F.3d 1053, 1057 (9th Cir., 2012).

139. Gay Student Services v. Texas A&M University, 737 F.2d 1317 (5th Cir., 1984); University of Southern Mississippi Chapter of the Mississippi Civil Liberties Union v. University of Southern Mississippi, 452 F.2d 564 (5th Cir., 1971).

140. Elizabeth Redden, "Pro-Palestinian Group Banned on Political Grounds," *Inside Higher Ed* ( January 18, 2017).

141. Bazaar v. Fortune, 476 F.2d 570, 580 (5th Cir., 1973).

142. Gay Alliance of Students v. Matthews, 544 F.2d 162, 168 (4th Cir., 1976).

143. Gay Lesbian Bisexual Alliance v. Pryor, 110 F.3d 1543 (11th Cir., 1997).

144. Matthew Kelly, "SGA's Decision Not to Recognize Young Americans for Liberty Group Creates National Backlash," *Wichita State Sunflower* (April 8, 2017).

145. Robby Soave, "Pomona College Students Say There's No Such Thing As Truth, 'Truth' Is a Tool of White Supremacy," *Hit & Run Blog, Reason.com* (April 17, 2017).

146. "Wellesley Statement from CERE Faculty re: Laura Kipnis Freedom Project Visit and Aftermath," Foundation for Individual Rights in Education, Fire.com (March 20, 2017).

147. "Free Speech Is Not Violated at Wellesley," *Wellesley News* (April 12, 2017).

148. "Wellesley Statement from CERE Faculty re: Laura Kipnis Freedom Project Visit and Aftermath."

149. Eugene Volokh, "Texas Legislator Shouted Down at Texas Southern University Law School," *Washington Post* (October 10, 2017); Jeremy Bauer-Wolf, "Free Speech Tour Halted at American University," *Inside Higher Ed* (September 29, 2017).

150. Aaron Hanlon, "What Stunts Like Milo Yiannopoulos's 'Free Speech Week' Cost," *New York Times* (September 24, 2017); Hannah Natanson and Derek G. Xiao, "At Harvard, Free Speech Likely Costs Thousands," *Harvard Crimson* (October 12, 2017); Robin Hattersley-Gray, "University of Utah Might Bill Students for Controversial Speaker Security," *Campus Safety* (October 10, 2017); Paige Fry, "State of Emergency Declared Ahead of UF White Nationalist Speech," *Palm Beach Post* (October 17, 2017).

151. Nick Roll, "UVA Releases Assessment on White Nationalist March," *Inside Higher Ed* (September 12, 2017).

152. Cliff Pinckard, "Lawyer Threatens to Sue Ohio State University over Richard Spencer Event," Cleveland.com (October 18, 2017); Chris Joyner, "Are Georgia Colleges Ready for Alt-Right Rallies?," *Atlanta Journal-Constitution* (April 20, 2017); Annalisa Merelli, "The University of Florida Is Allowing Richard Spencer to Speak Because It Has To," *Quartz* (October 17, 2017).

153. Courts have often found that the ability of universities, particularly state universities, to restrict access to campus by members of the general public who wish to express themselves is somewhat limited. See, e.g., State of New Jersey v. Schmid, 84 N.J. 535 (N.J., 1980); Board of Trustees of the State University of New York v. Fox, 492

U.S. 469 (1989); McGlone v. Bell, 681 F.3d 718 (6th Cir., 2012); Bloedorn v. Grube, 631 F.3d 1218 (11th Cir., 2011); Brister v. Faulkner, 214 F.3d 675 (5th Cir., 2000).

154. American Association of University Professors, "1940 Statement of Principles on Academic Freedom and Tenure" (https://www.aaup.org/file/1940%20Statement .pdf).

155. Quoted in Matthew W. Finkin and Robert C. Post, *For the Common Good* (New Haven, CT: Yale University Press, 2009), 31, 4, 64.

156. Robert O'Neil, *Academic Freedom in the Wired World* (Cambridge, MA: Harvard University Press, 2008), 1–8.

157. John R. Silber, "Poisoning the Wells of Academe," *Encounter* 43 (August 1974): 37.

158. Sandra Y. L. Korn, "The Doctrine of Academic Freedom," *Harvard Crimson* (February 18, 2014).

159. https://new.oberlin.edu/petition-jan2016.pdf

160. "Students Demand Power over Hiring after Job Offer to 'Racist' White Professor," *Claremont Independent* (April 21, 2017).

161. Conor Friedersdorf, "The New Intolerance of Student Activism," *Atlantic* (November 9, 2015).

162. Tom Bartlett, "Star Scholar Resigns from Northwestern, Saying It Doesn't Respect Academic Freedom," *Chronicle of Higher Education* (August 26, 2015); Peter Schmidt, "Northwestern U. Is Accused of Violating Academic Freedom," *Chronicle of Higher Education* (March 3, 2017).

163. Colleen Flaherty, "White Is the Word," *Inside Higher Ed* (January 18, 2017).

164. Scott Jaschik, "Who Is Being Political?," *Inside Higher Ed* (February 19, 2015); Rick Seltzer, "Silencing Advocacy That Irritates State Leaders," *Inside Higher Ed* (February 28, 2017); Nick Roll, "UNC Board Bars Litigation by Law School Center," *Inside Higher Ed* (September 11, 2017).

165. Molly Corbett Broad, "We All Could Lose in UVa Case," *Inside Higher Ed* (July 29, 2010); Scott Jaschik, "Off Limits," *Inside Higher Ed* (March 5, 2012); Greg Grieco, "Professors Association: Defend Academic Freedom," *Philly.com* (February 2, 2017).

166. AAUP Committee A, quoted in Finkin and Post, *For the Common Good*, 142–143.

167. Scott Jaschik, "Fireable Tweets," *Inside Higher Ed* (December 19, 2013); Erik Voeten, "Kansas Board of Regents Restricts Free Speech for Academics," *Washington Post* (December 19, 2013); Colleen Flaherty, "Protected Tweet?," *Inside Higher Ed* (September 23, 2013).

168. Ellie Bothwell, "University of British Columbia Chair Resigns over Academic Freedom Case," *Times Higher Education* (October 19, 2015).

169. Peter Schmidt, "Professors Fault Virginia Tech's Tepid Defense of Colleague Caught Up in Free-Speech Controversy," *Chronicle of Higher Education* (November 25, 2013).

170. Salaita had written, for example, that "I wish all the fucking West Bank set-

tlers would go missing," that "if Netanyahu appeared on TV with a necklace made from the teeth of Palestinian children, would anyone be surprised," that "Zionists" bore responsibility for "eagerly conflating Jewishness and Israel" and thus "transforming 'anti-Semitism' from something horrible into something honorable since 1948." Quoted in Cary Nelson, "An Appointment to Reject," *Inside Higher Ed* (August 8, 2014).

171. Christine Des Garennes, "Updated: Wise Explains Salaita Decision, Gets Support from Trustees," *Champaign News-Gazette* (August, 23, 2014).

172. Nelson, "An Appointment to Reject."

173. Hank Reichman, "Bérubé on Salaita," *Academe Blog* (August 7, 2014) (https://academeblog.org/2014/08/07/berube-on-salaita/).

174. Corey Robin, "Reading the Salaita Papers," *Crooked Timber* (September 3, 2014) (http://crookedtimber.org/2014/09/03/reading-the-salaita-papers/).

175. Conor Friedersdorf, "Stripping a Professor of Tenure over a Blog Post," *Atlantic* (February 9, 2015).

176. Colleen Flaherty, "Looking into Tweets," *Inside Higher Ed* (April 18, 2017).

177. Colleen Flaherty, "Texas A&M Softens Tone toward Professor," *Inside Higher Ed* (May 18, 2017).

## Chapter 4. Ideological Ostracism and Viewpoint Diversity on Campus

1. David Glenn, "Senator Proposes an End to Federal Support for Political Science," *Chronicle of Higher Education* (October 7, 2009).

2. See, e.g., Neil Gross, *Why Are Professors Liberal and Why Do Conservatives Care?* (Cambridge, MA: Harvard University Press, 2013); Daniel B. Klein and Charlotta Stern, "Professors and Their Politics: The Policy Views of Social Scientists," *Critical Review* 17 (2005): 257; Christopher F. Cardiff and Daniel B. Klein, "Faculty Partisan Affiliations in All Disciplines: A Voter-Registration Study," *Critical Review* 17 (2005): 237; Stanley Rothman, S. Robert Lichter, and Neil Nevitte, "Politics and Professional Advancement among College Faculty," *Forum* 3 (2005); Jon A. Shields and Joshua M. Dunn Sr., *Passing on the Right* (New York: Oxford University Press, 2016); Samuel J. Abrams, "The Contented Professors: How Conservative Faculty See Themselves within the Academy" (2016) (https://www.researchgate.net/profile/Samuel_Abrams/publication/312229229_The_Contented_Professors_How_Conservative_Faculty_See_Themselves_within_the_Academy/links/58778fea08ae6eb871d152c6/The-Contented-Professors-How-Conservative-Faculty-See-Themselves-within-the-Academy.pdf).

3. Ernest O. Melby, "Proving the Critics' Case," *Inside Higher Ed* (August 26, 2005); "Debating Party Parity in Faculty Population," *Duke Magazine* (June 1, 2004); Grover Furr, "'Left' Professorate? If It Only Were...," H-HOAC Discussion Logs (November 19, 2004) (http://h-net.msu.edu/cgi-bin/logbrowse.pl?trx=vx&list=h-hoac&month=0411&week=c&msg=j15TAqkdMYr/Z5vq/wu7yA&user=&pw=);

Jennifer Jacobson, "Conservatives in a Liberal Landscape," *Chronicle of Higher Education* (September 24, 2004).

4. Allison Stanger, "Understanding the Angry Mob at Middlebury That Gave Me a Concussion," *New York Times* (March 13, 2017); Wendy M. Williams and Stephen J. Ceci, "Charles Murray's 'Provocative' Talk," *New York Times* (April 15, 2017).

5. Scott Jaschik, "Middlebury Professor Sorry for Co-Sponsoring Murray Talk," *Inside Higher Ed* (April 26, 2017).

6. Scott Jaschik, "Torture and Tenure," *Inside Higher Ed* (April 14, 2008).

7. Christopher Edley, Jr., "The Torture Memos and Academic Freedom" (April 10, 2008) (https://www.law.berkeley.edu/article/the-torture-memos-and-academic -freedom/).

8. Brian Leiter, "Freedom to Be Wrong," *New York Times* (August 20, 2009).

9. "Thought Crimes Watch: Comparing Trans-Racialism to Transgenderism Verboten!" *Leiter Reports* (May 1, 2017) (http://leiterreports.typepad.com/blog/2017/05 /thought-crimes-watch-comparing-trans-racialism-to-transgenderism-verboten .html#more).

10. "Open Letter to Hypatia" (https://docs.google.com/forms/d/1efp9C0MHch _6Kfgtlm0PZ76nirWtcEsqWHcvgidl2mU/viewform?ts=59066d20&edit_requested =true).

11. "Nora Berenstain on Rebecca Tuvel and Hypatia," GenderTrender (April 29, 2017) (https://gendertrender.wordpress.com/nora-berenstain-on-rebecca-tuvel -and-hypatia/); Lindsay McKenzie, Adam Harris, and Fernanda Zamudio-Suarez, "A Journal Article Provoked a Schism in Philosophy; Now the Rifts Are Deepening," *Chronicle of Higher Education* (May 6, 2017).

12. Kelly Oliver, "If This Is Feminism . . . ," *Philosophical Salon* (May 8, 2017) (http://thephilosophicalsalon.com/if-this-is-feminism-its-been-hijacked-by-the -thought-police/).

13. Jesse Singal, "This Is What a Modern-Day Witch Hunt Looks Like," *New York Magazine* (May 2, 2017); José Luis Bermúdez, "Defining 'Hate' in the Tuvel Affair," *Inside Higher Ed* (May 5, 2017); "The Defamation of Rebecca Tuvel by the Board of Associate Editors of Hypatia and the Authors of the Open Letter," *Leiter Reports* (May 1, 2017) (http://leiterreports.typepad.com/blog/2017/05/the-defamation-of-rebecca -tuvel-by-the-board-of-associate-editors-of-hypatia-and-the-open-letter.html); Oliver, "If This is Feminism . . .".

14. McKenzie, Harris, and Zamudio-Suarez, "A Journal Article Provoked a Schism in Philosophy."

15. Colleen Flaherty, "A Dangerous Withdrawal," *Inside Higher Ed* (October 9, 2017).

16. Chris Quintana, "Drexel Puts Professor on Leave after Tweet about Las Vegas Draws Conservative Ire," *Chronicle of Higher Education* (October 10, 2017).

17. Anemona Hartocollis, "A Campus Argument Goes Viral. Now the College Is under Siege," *New York Times* (June 16, 2017).

18. Cardiff and Klein, "Faculty Partisan Affiliations in All Disciplines," 247; James

Lindgren, "Measuring Diversity: Law Faculties in 1997 and 2012," *Harvard Journal of Law & Public Policy* 39 (2016): 89; John O. McGinnis, Matthew A. Schwartz, and Benjamin Tisdell, "The Patterns and Implications of Political Contributions by Elite Law School Faculty," *Georgetown Law Journal* 93 (2005): 1167; Adam Bonica, Adam Chilton, Kyle Rozema, and Maya Sen, "The Legal Academy's Ideological Uniformity" (2017) (https://ssrn.com/abstract=2953087).

19. Bonica, Chilton, Rozema, and Sen, "The Legal Academy's Ideological Uniformity."

20. "San Francisco Affirmative Litigation Project" (https://law.yale.edu/studying-law-yale/clinical-and-experiential-learning/our-clinics/san-francisco-affirmative-litigation-project).

21. "Death Penalty Clinic" (https://www.law.berkeley.edu/experiential/clinics/death-penalty-clinic/about-the-clinic/).

22. Steven M. Teles, *The Rise of the Conservative Legal Movement* (Princeton, NJ: Princeton University Press, 2008); Amanda Hollis-Brusky, *Ideas with Consequences* (New York: Oxford University Press, 2015).

23. Randy Barnett, "Our Letter to the Association of American Law Schools," *Washington Post* (February 25, 2017).

24. Far better that such political backlash take the form of legislative efforts to secure general free speech protections than that of legislative micromanaging of university policies and personnel, but better still if universities deflected such efforts by securing free speech on their own. Collen Flaherty, "Tennessee Free Speech Bill Signed into Law," *Inside Higher Ed* (May 11, 2017). In the early 2000s, the conservative activist David Horowitz promoted an "Academic Bill of Rights" that would have required by law that universities make hiring decisions so as to promote "a plurality of methodologies and perspectives" and include in course syllabi "dissenting sources and viewpoints." Such ham-handed efforts to politically intervene in how scholarship is pursued and taught is ultimately subversive of maintaining institutions dedicated to free inquiry in accord with professional scholarly standards, but it should not be surprising if conservative students, activists, and politicians question how well universities are adhering to their stated mission of open inquiry when the range of scholarship seems stunted. Scott Jaschik, "More Criticism of 'Academic Bill of Rights,'" *Inside Higher Ed* (January 9, 2006).

25. Jeremiah B. Wills, Zachary W. Brewster, Jonathan R. Brauer, and Bradley Ray, "Political Ideological Distance between Sociology Students and Their Instructors: The Effects of Students' Perceptions," *Sociation Today* 11 (2013); Susan Bullers, Melissa Reece, and Christy Skinner, "Political Ideology and Perceptions of Bias among University Faculty," *Sociation Today* 8 (2010); Stanley Rothman, S. Robert Lichter, and Neil Nevitte, "Politics and Professional Advancement among College Faculty," *Forum* 3 (2005); April Kelly-Woessner and Matthew Woessner, "My Professor Is a Partisan Hack: How Perceptions of a Professor's Political Views Affect Student Course Evaluations," *PS* 39 (2006): 495.

26. John K. Wilson, *The Myth of Political Correctness* (Durham, NC: Duke Univer-

sity Press, 1995); Eric Alterman, "Who's behind the Right-Wing Assault on Public Universities," *Nation* (September 1, 2016); Christopher Mele, "Professor Watchlist Is Seen as Threat to Academic Freedom," *New York Times* (November 28, 2016).

27. Robert Maranto and Matthew Woessner, "Why Conservative Fears of Campus Indoctrination Are Overblown," *Chronicle of Higher Education* (July 31, 2017); Scott Jaschik, "Tolerant Faculty, Intolerant Students," *Inside Higher Ed* (August 20, 2008); Scott Jaschik, "Stop Blaming Professors," *Inside Higher Ed* (June 10, 2014).

# FOR FURTHER READING

Some useful studies of the life of the American mind and its institutional and cultural underpinnings include Jacques Barzun, *The House of Intellect* (Chicago: University of Chicago Press, 1959); Richard Hofstadter, *Anti-Intellectualism in American Life* (New York: Alfred A. Knopf, 1963); Merle Curti, *The Growth of American Thought*, 3rd ed. (New York: Harper & Row, 1964); Perry Miller, *The Life of the Mind in America* (New York: Harcourt, Brace & World, 1965); Clement Eaton, *The Mind of the Old South*, rev. ed. (Baton Rouge: Louisiana State University Press, 1967); Allan Bloom, *The Closing of the American Mind* (New York: Simon Schuster, 1987); Lewis Perry, *Intellectual Life in America* (Chicago: University of Chicago Press, 1989); Dane S. Claussen, *Anti-Intellectualism in American Media* (New York: Peter Lang, 2003); Susan Jacoby, *The Age of American Unreason* (New York: Vintage, 2009); Daniel Walker Howe, *Making the American Self* (New York: Oxford University Press, 2009).

On the challenges confronting contemporary higher education, see William G. Bowen, Martin A. Kurzwell, and Eugene M. Tobin, *Equity and Excellence in American Higher Education* (Charlottesville: University of Virginia Press, 2005); Christopher Newfield, *Unmaking the Public University* (Cambridge, MA: Harvard University Press, 2008); Gaye Tuchman, *Wannabe U* (Chicago: University of Chicago Press, 2009);

Ellen Schrecker, *The Lost Soul of Higher Education* (New York: New Press, 2010); Richard Arum and Josipa Roksa, *Academically Adrift* (Chicago: University of Chicago Press, 2011); Benjamin Ginsberg, *The Fall of the Faculty* (New York: Oxford University Press, 2011); Derek Bok, *Higher Education in America* (Princeton, NJ: Princeton University Press, 2013); Suzanne Mettler, *Degrees of Inequality* (New York: Basic Books, 2014); Larry G. Geber, *The Rise and Decline of Faculty Governance* (Baltimore: Johns Hopkins University Press, 2014); Goldie Blumenstyk, *American Higher Education in Crisis?* (New York: Oxford University Press, 2014); William G. Bowen and Eugene M. Tobin, *Locus of Authority* (Princeton, NJ: Princeton University Press, 2015); John McGee, *Breakpoint* (Baltimore: Johns Hopkins University Press, 2015); Tressie McMillan Cottom, *Lower Ed: The Troubling Rise of For-Profit Colleges in the New Economy* (New York: The New Press, 2017).

On the development of American colleges over time, see Laurence R. Veysey, *The Emergence of the American University* (Chicago: University of Chicago Press, 1965); Christopher Jencks and David Riesman, *The Academic Revolution* (Garden City, NY: Doubleday, 1968); Robert Nisbet, *The Degradation of Academic Dogma* (New York: Basic Books, 1971); John S. Brubacher and Willis Rudy, *Higher Education in Transition* (New York: Harper & Row, 1976); David O. Levine, *The American College and the Culture of Aspiration, 1915–1940* (Ithaca, NY: Cornell University Press, 1986); Frederick Rudolph, *The American College and University* (Athens: University of Georgia Press, 1990); Clark Kerr, *The Great Transformation in Higher Education, 1960–1980* (Albany: State University of New York Press, 1991); Julie A. Reuben, *The Making of the Modern University* (Chicago: University of Chicago Press, 1996); John R. Thelin, *A History of American Higher Education* (Baltimore:

Johns Hopkins University Press, 2004); Larry G. Gerber, *The Rise and Decline of Faculty Governance* (Baltimore: Johns Hopkins University Press, 2014).

Some useful discourses on the purposes of a university include John Henry Newman, *The Idea of a University* (New York: Longmans, Green, and Co., 1891); Alexander Meiklejohn, *The Liberal College* (Boston: Marshall Jones Company, 1920); Clark Kerr, *The Uses of the University* (Cambridge, MA: Harvard University Press, 1963); Robert Paul Wolff, *The Ideal of the University* (Boston: Beacon Press, 1969); Derek Bok, *Beyond the Ivory Tower* (Cambridge, MA: Harvard University Press, 1982); Thomas Erlich, *The Courage to Inquire* (Bloomington: Indiana University Press, 1995); Christopher J. Lucas, *Crisis in the Academy* (New York: St. Martin's Press, 1996); Bill Readings, *The University in Ruins* (Cambridge, MA: Harvard University Press, 1996); Donald Kennedy, *Academic Duty* (Cambridge, MA: Harvard University Press, 1997); Zachary Karabell, *What's College For?* (New York: Basic Books, 1998); James O. Freedman, *Liberal Education and the Public Interest* (Iowa City: University of Iowa Press, 2003); Richard Levin, *The Work of the University* (New Haven, CT: Yale University Press, 2003); Harold T. Shapiro, *A Larger Sense of Purpose* (Princeton, NJ: Princeton University Press, 2005).

The literature on free speech principles is voluminous. Much of it has been developed in the particular context of constitutional law and legal protections for free speech, but scholars working on these issues have frequently traversed back and forth between specifically constitutional principles and more broadly philosophical principles. Some particularly notable general works include Zechariah Chafee Jr., *Freedom of Speech* (New York: Harcourt, Brace and Howe, 1920); Alexander Meiklejohn, *Political Freedom* (New York: Harper & Brothers,

1948); Thomas I. Emerson, *The System of Freedom of Expression* (New York: Vintage, 1970); Frederick Schauer, *Free Speech* (New York: Cambridge University Press, 1982); Martin H. Redish, *Freedom of Expression* (Charlottesville, VA: Michie Co., 1984); Harry Kalven Jr., *A Worthy Tradition* (New York: Harper & Row, 1988); C. Edwin Baker, *Human Liberty and Freedom of Speech* (New York: Oxford University Press, 1989); Owen M. Fiss, *The Irony of Free Speech* (Cambridge, MA: Harvard University Press, 1996); Cass R. Sunstein, *Why Societies Need Dissent* (Cambridge, MA: Harvard University Press, 2003). Some more historical works include Paul L. Murphy, *The Meaning of Free Speech* (Westport, CT: Greenwood Publishing, 1972); Leonard W. Levy, *Emergence of a Free Press* (New York: Oxford University Press, 1985); Mark A. Graber, *Transforming Free Speech* (Berkeley: University of California Press, 1991); Margaret A. Blanchard, *Revolutionary Sparks* (New York: Oxford University Press, 1992); David M. Rabban, *Free Speech in Its Forgotten Years* (New York: Cambridge University Press, 1997); Michael Kent Curtis, *Free Speech, "The People's Darling Privilege"* (Durham, NC: Duke University Press, 2000); Geoffrey R. Stone, *Perilous Times* (New York: W. W. Norton, 2004); Stephen M. Feldman, *Free Expression and Democracy in America* (Chicago: University of Chicago Press, 2008).

The literature on academic freedom has come in waves since the early twentieth century. Some notable contributions include Charles W. Eliot, *Academic Freedom* (Ithaca, NY: n.p., 1907); American Association of University Professors, *Report of the Committee on Academic Freedom and Academic Tenure* (Boston: n.p., 1915); Richard Hofstadter and Walter P. Metzger, *The Development of Academic Freedom in the United States* (New York: Columbia University Press, 1955); Hans W. Baade, ed., *Academic Freedom* (Dobbs Ferry, NY: Oceana Publications, 1964); Sidney Hooke, *In Defense of Academic Freedom* (New York: Pegasus, 1971); Matthew W. Finkin and Robert C. Post, *For the Common Good* (New Haven, CT: Yale University Press, 2000); Donald Alexander Downs, *Restoring Free Speech and Liberty on Campus* (New York: Cambridge University Press, 2005); Joan Delfattore, *Knowledge in the Making* (New Haven, CT: Yale University Press, 2010); Robert C. Post, *Democracy, Expertise, and Academic Freedom* (New Haven, CT: Yale University Press, 2012); Greg Lukianoff, *Unlearning Liberty* (New York: Encounter Books, 2012); Paul Horwitz, *First Amendment Institutions* (Cambridge, MA: Harvard University Press, 2013); Stanley Fish, *Versions of Academic Freedom* (Chicago: University of Chicago Press, 2014); Jonathan Rauch, *Kindly Inquisitors*, rev. ed. (Chicago: University of Chicago Press, 2014); Frank Furedi, *What's Happened to the University?* (New York: Routledge, 2016); Erwin Chemerinsky and Howard Gillman, *Free Speech on Campus* (New Haven, CT: Yale University Press, 2017).

The tension between freedom of speech and concerns about equality and inclusion has received particular attention in recent years. Some notable works examining that problem include Joel Feinberg, *Offense to Others* (New York: Oxford University Press, 1985); Catharine MacKinnon, *Only Words* (Cambridge, MA: Harvard University Press, 1993); Mari J. Matsuda, Charles R. Lawrence III, Richard Delgado, and Kimberle Williams, *Words That Wound* (Boulder, CO: Westview Press, 1993); Franklyn S. Haiman, *"Speech Acts" and the First Amendment* (Carbondale: Southern Illinois University Press, 1993); Samuel Walker, *Hate Speech* (Lincoln: University of Nebraska Press, 1994); Kent Greenawalt, *Fighting Words* (Princeton, NJ: Princeton University Press, 1995); James Weinstein, *Hate Speech, Pornography, and the Radical Attack on Free Speech Doctrine* (Boulder, CO: Westview Press, 1999); Laura Beth Nielsen, *License to Harass* (Princeton, NJ: Princeton University Press, 2004); Jon B. Gould, *Speak No Evil* (Chicago: University of Chicago Press, 2005); Stephen J. Heyman, *Free Speech and Human Dignity* (New Haven, CT: Yale University Press, 2008); Timothy C. Shiell, *Campus Hate Speech on Trial*, rev. ed. (Lawrence: University Press of Kansas, 2009); Ivan Hare and James Weinstein, eds., *Extreme Speech and Democracy* (New York: Oxford University Press, 2011); Ishani Maitra and Mary Kate McGowan, eds., *Speech and Harm* (New York: Oxford University Press, 2012); Jeremy Waldron, *The Harm in Hate Speech* (Cambridge, MA: Harvard University Press, 2012); Michael Herz and Peter Molnar, eds., *The Content and Context of Hate Speech* (New York: Cambridge University Press, 2012); Timothy Garton Ash, *Free Speech* (New Haven, CT: Yale University Press, 2016); Sigal R. Ben-Porath, *Free Speech on Campus* (Philadelphia: University of Pennsylvania Press, 2017).

# INDEX

*Abrams v. United States*, 45
academic freedom, 5–7, 21–24, 48–49, 57, 66, 141–151, 153, 154–155, 156–157, 159, 165, 169–170
Adams, Henry, 10
Adams, John, 32
*The Adventures of Huckleberry Finn*, 63
Air Force Academy, 73
Albert, Michael, 138
Albright, Madeleine, 118
Alien and Sedition Acts of 1798, 32–36
American Association of University Professors (AAUP), 53–54, 64–65, 77, 141–142, 146–147, 148, 151, 156
American Civil Liberties Union (ACLU), 109
American University, 139
Amherst College, 22
Angell, James B., 21
anti-intellectualism, 9–10
Association of American Law Schools (AALS), 175
Australia, 64, 108

Berdahl, Jennifer, 154–155
Bethune-Cookman University, 120–121
Big Sean, 118
Birgeneau, Robert, 120
Black Justice League, 96–97, 104
Black Lives Matter, 92, 109
Bowdoin College, 72
Bowen, William, 120
British Union of Fascists, 109
Bruce, Lenny, 131
Buckley, William F., 22–23, 27
Bush, George W., 168
Butler, Samuel, 10

By Any Means Necessary (BAMN), 100, 102, 105

California Institute of Technology (Caltech), 13
Canada, 110, 154–155
Cardiff University, 109
Carlin, George, 58–59, 131
Carnegie, Andrew, 20
Carnegie University, 21
censorship, 30–46, 52, 58, 74, 83–92, 97, 113, 127, 129, 132–136, 148–150, 167–168, 170–172
Central Connecticut State College, 125
Chaplinsky, Walter, 80–81
*Chaplinsky v. New Hampshire*, 80–81
*Charlie Hebdo*, 131
Chomsky, Noam, 137
Christakis, Nicholas, 149
Ciccariello-Maher, George, 158–159, 172
civility, 47, 71, 73, 82, 84, 93, 97–98, 156, 176
Claremont McKenna College, 108, 134
Clay, Andrew Dice, 131
Clinton, Hillary, 117
Coalition for Oxy for Diversity and Equity, 120
Coburn, Tom, 165
Cohn, Ernst, 2–3
College of William & Mary, 109
College Republicans, 128–129, 145
Collins, Patricia Hill, 84
Columbia University, 109
commencement speakers, 117–122
Commission for Ethnicity, Race, and Equity, 135–136

Concerned Student 1950, 101
conformity, 3, 4, 37–38, 43, 119, 146, 148, 150–152, 153–154, 162
Cornell University, 21
Cosby, Bill, 117
Cotton, John, 37
Coulter, Ann, 85, 92, 131, 133, 145, 167
Cronkite, Walter, 26
Curry, Tommy, 159

Dean, Howard, 78, 80
DeGraff, Howard, 143
Derrida, Jacques, 84
DeVos, Betsy, 22, 27, 120–121
Dewey, John, 54
Dickinson College, 90
disruptive protests, 99–106
Douglass, Frederick, 9
Draper, Andrew S., 21
Dreger, Alice, 149–150
Drexel University, 158–159, 172
Duke University, 75

Edison, Thomas, 9
Eliot, Charles, 21
Emerson, Thomas, 113–114
Emory University, 70
Evergreen College, 172
extramural speech, 150–160

Federalist Society, 139, 174–175
Finley, Karen, 131
Fish, Stanley, 26
Flynt, Larry, 131
Fordham University, 126
Foucault, Michel, 65–66, 84
Foundation for Individual Rights in Education (FIRE), 121
freedom of thought, 24, 36–37
free speech, justifications for, 6–7, 19–20, 28–30, 36–37, 39–47, 49–50, 53–57, 79–80, 86–87, 99, 115–116, 131–133

Gay Alliance of Students, 127, 130
Gay Lesbian Bisexual Alliance, 128
Gay Student Services, 125
George Washington University, 72

Gilman, Daniel Coit, 21
Goffman, Alice, 149
Goldman, Emma, 85
Goldsmiths, University of London, 110
Great Britain, 74
*The Great Gatsby*, 63
Greer, Germaine, 109
Gupta, Arvind, 154

Harvard University, 12, 21, 72, 103–104, 110, 148
hate speech, 77–94
Haverford College, 120
heckler's veto, 99, 112–114
Hofstadter, Richard, 9
Holmes, Oliver Wendell, 45–46
Hutchinson, Robert Maynard, 25
*Hypatia*, 170–171

indoctrination, 3, 21, 22–23, 24, 29, 102, 171, 177

Jefferson, Thomas, 30, 32
Jobs, Steve, 9
Johns Hopkins University, 21

Kennedy, Christopher, 156
Kennedy, Randall, 120
King, Martin Luther, Jr., 9, 104–105
King's College London, 90
Kipnis, Laura, 134–135, 136–137

Lehigh University, 66
Leiter, Brian, 24, 169–170
liberalism, 8, 21, 23–24, 29, 30–31, 36–39, 86, 102, 105–106, 113–114, 116, 131, 136, 159–160, 162
Liberty University, 13
Lincoln, Abraham, 9
Locke, John, 36, 37, 136
London School of Economics, 90

Mac Donald, Heather, 108, 134
*Mad*, 131
Madison, James, 32
Malcolm X, 85
Mann, Michael, 150
Mansfield, Harvey, 148

Marcuse, Herbert, 23–24, 27
marketplace of ideas, 45–46, 98, 126
Marquette University, 158
Matsuda, Mari, 89, 91
McConaughey, Matthew, 117
McInnes, Gavin, 108
McMaster University, 110
Meiklejohn, Alexander, 22
Michigan State University, 72
Middlebury College, 5, 107–108, 110,
 111, 161, 167–168
Mill, John Stuart, 37–39, 46–49, 76,
 98, 115, 133, 136, 163; Mill's argu-
 ment from arrogance, 41–42; Mill's
 argument from conviction, 42–44;
 Mill's argument from humility, 39–
 41, 45
Milton, John, 31, 36, 45, 136
Mississippi Civil Liberties Union, 126
Montalbano, John, 154–155
More, Paul Elmore, 10
Murray, Charles, 92, 107–108, 110,
 167–168

Nation, Carrie, 1–2, 80
*National Review*, 23
National Rifle Association, 152–153
Navarro, Peter, 137–138
Nearing, Scott, 143, 144
Nelson, Cary, 156–157
New York University, 108
Nixon, Richard, 114
Northwestern University, 108–109, 135,
 137, 149–150
Notre Dame University, 121, 122, 161

Obama, Barack, 117, 120
Oberlin College, 64, 148–149, 162
obstructionist protests, 99, 106–116,
 167–168
Occidental College, 25, 64, 109–110
Occupy Wall Street, 138
Ohio State University, 103–104
Oregon State University, 125
Oz, Mehmet, 138

Paulsen, Friedrich, 53
Pence, Mike, 117, 121, 122

Peterson, Jordan, 110
Pomona College, 134, 138, 149
Post, Robert C., 49
post-traumatic stress disorder (PTSD),
 59–63
Princeton University, 12, 21, 96, 104,
 118, 120
public forum doctrine, 123–125

*R.A.V. v. St. Paul*, 79, 86
Reclaim Harvard Law, 103, 106
Reed College, 108, 110, 162
Reich, Robert, 137
Rice, Condoleezza, 118
Roosevelt, Franklin D., 81
Ross, Edward A., 142, 143, 147
Rutgers University, 118

safe spaces, 66–77
Salaita, Steven, 155–157
Sarah Lawrence College, 13
Savio, Mario, 105
Schockley, William, 54–55
Singer, Peter, 108, 110, 111, 112
Snooki, 117
Socialist Alternative, 145
Sowell, Thomas, 138
speech as violence, 83–85
speech codes, 82, 88–90
Spelman College, 13
Spencer, Richard, 133
Stanford, Jane, 142
Stanford University, 21, 142, 147
Stanger, Allison, 107–108
Stern, Howard, 131
Stone, Geoffrey R., 55–56
Students for a Democratic Society, 125
Students for Justice in Palestine, 108,
 126
Students Supporting Israel, 108
Supreme Court, US, 34, 49, 79, 81, 82,
 84, 95, 114, 123, 125
Swarthmore College, 13

tenure, 146–148, 149, 152, 158, 168–169
Terminiello, Arthur, 81–82
*Terminiello v. Chicago*, 81–82
Texas A&M University, 125, 159

Texas Southern University, 139
time, place, and manner regulations, 95–96, 124
Tocqueville, Alexis de, 38
tolerance, 8, 23–24, 29, 36–39, 47, 73–74, 77, 86, 115–116, 120, 127, 131, 162, 176, 178
trigger warnings, 57–66
Trump, Donald, 85, 92, 110, 137–138
Trump, Donald, Jr., 117
Tuvel, Rebecca, 170–171

universities: benefits of, 16–18; inclusivity of, 19, 47, 73–75, 95, 163; mission of, 12–16, 18, 19–22, 25–26; problems of, 10–11
University College London, 90
University of Breslau, 2–3
University of British Columbia (UBC), 154–155
University of California at Berkeley, 1–2, 5, 100, 105, 110, 111, 120, 168–169
University of California at Irvine, 137
University of California at Santa Barbara, 108
University of Chicago, 25, 55–56
University of Illinois, 21, 84, 155–157, 161
University of Kansas, 152–153
University of Michigan, 21, 88, 89, 91
University of Mississippi, 127
University of Missouri, 101, 143
University of North Carolina, 76, 150
University of Pennsylvania, 142–143
University of Southern Alabama, 128
University of Southern Mississippi, 125–126

University of Texas, 13, 26
University of Toronto, 110
University of Victoria, 108, 110
University of Virginia, 125, 140
University of West Florida, 13
University of Wisconsin, 21, 89–90

Van Zandt, Steven, 118
Veitch, Jonathan, 119–120
viewpoint diversity, 163–178
Virginia Commonwealth University, 127, 130, 132
Virginia Tech University, 155
Virginia v. Black, 79

Wallace, George, 54
Washington, George, 9, 32
Weaver, Richard, 10
Webb, Jim, 117
Weinstein, Bret, 172
Wellesley College, 64, 135, 136–137, 138
Welsing, Frances Cress, 55
Wharton, Joseph, 144
Whitney v. California, 79–80
Wichita State University, 129–130
Williams, Roger, 37
Wilson, Woodrow, 21
Wise, Phyllis, 155–156
Wolfe, Tim, 101
Woodward, C. Vann, 55

Yale University, 12, 21, 23, 54–55, 115, 149
Yiannopoulos, Milo, 2, 85, 108, 110, 111, 131, 132
Yoo, John, 168–169
Young Americans for Liberty, 130, 132, 139